POST-REVOLUTIONARY NICARAGUA

**California Series on
Social Choice and Political Economy**

Edited by Brian Barry and Samuel L. Popkin

POST-REVOLUTIONARY NICARAGUA

STATE, CLASS, AND THE DILEMMAS OF AGRARIAN POLICY

Forrest D. Colburn

UNIVERSITY OF CALIFORNIA PRESS

Berkeley   Los Angeles   London

University of California Press
Berkeley and Los Angeles, California

University of California Press, Ltd.
London, England

© 1986 by
The Regents of the University of California

Library of Congress Cataloging in Publication Data

Colburn, Forrest D.
    Post-Revolutionary Nicaragua.

    Bibliography: p.
    Includes index.
    1. Agriculture—Economic aspects—Nicaragua.
2. Nicaragua—Rural conditions. 3. Nicaragua—Politics
and government—1979–   . 4. Social classes—
Nicaragua. I. Title.
HD1817.C63   1986   338.1′097285   85–5798
ISBN 0–520–05524–1

Printed in the United States of America

1   2   3   4   5   6   7   8   9

HD
1817
C43
1986

a los nicaragüenses
absit invidia

MAR 20 '87

WITHDRAWN

100129

EMORY AND HENRY LIBRARY

Contents

List of Tables

Acknowledgments

Many individuals contributed to the research and analysis that made this work possible. Norman Uphoff, Milton Esman, Marc Lindenberg, Silvio De Franco, Rodrigo Cantarero, Silvio Morales, and Juan Guerrero deserve special mention. The manuscript has benefited from comments provided by Robert Bates, Martin Bernal, Caroline Ciancutti, Richard Feinberg, Allen Graubard, Lowell Gudmundson, and David Zweig. Field research was made possible by a fellowship from the Doherty Foundation, Princeton University, and by assistance from the Central American Institute of Business Administration. Institutional support was also provided by the Center for International Studies, Cornell University, and the Latin American and Caribbean Center, Florida International University.

Introduction

The Nicaraguan Revolution, led by the Sandinista Front for National Liberation (FSLN) and supported by a loose coalition drawn from every stratum of Nicaraguan society, toppled the Somoza dynasty in July of 1979, inspiring widespread hope that removal of the corrupt despot would make it possible to redress the many inequities in Nicaragua. That has not happened. The new regime has become bogged down in defending itself against a counterrevolution heavily supported by the United States. But even before armed resistance to the revolution began, the Nicaraguan regime was confronted with a host of economic constraints that have not only made it difficult to improve the welfare of lower classes but have also encouraged the adoption of policies inconsistent with revolutionary ideology, iconography, and phraseology.

The argument presented in this volume is that Nicaragua has been confronted with a rather predictable set of economic problems that beset contemporary post-revolutionary regimes in small developing countries. In small states like Nicaragua, economic problems have an unequaled immediacy because of a high dependence on imports and the resulting need to maintain exports at sufficient levels to prevent the disruption of consumption and investment. The urgency of Nicaragua's economic problems has prompted the new regime to offer concessions to those strata that generate foreign exchange and to concentrate state resources on foreign-exchange generation and on satisfaction of the consumption demands of the urban sector that is most important politically to the survival of the regime. The sector that has accordingly been "squeezed" in order to keep the revolution economically and politically solvent has been the rural producers—subsistence and small farmers, and agricultural laborers—who are not organized and do not control a vital foreign-exchange–producing crop.

This book is not intended to evaluate the outcome of the Nicaraguan Revolution. That would be presumptuous; it takes years, if not decades, for a revolution to run its course. Witness the Mexican Revolution of 1910–20, the first important revolution of the century: in the late 1920s, Mexico's government was little more than a frail dictatorship, but in the late 1930s it became a strong populist regime. Since 1940, the country has had a relatively benign authoritarian government. The Mexican economy did not recover from the losses and disruptions of the revolution until 1940, but from 1940 to 1970 the Mexican economy grew at an annual rate of almost 6.5 percent—a rate surpassed only by Japan and Finland among the nonsocialist developed nations and by a few advantaged countries (Libya, Korea, and Israel) in the developing world.

The aim here is to describe the intentions of the Sandinista revolutionary elite and to explain why their rosy expectations were dashed even before they were confronted with a U.S.-financed counterrevolution. This temporal focus is undertaken with the conviction that the initial years of post-revolutionary rule are decisive for regime survival, a point illustrated by regimes as disparate as Bolivia's Nationalist Revolutionary Movement and Allende's administration in Chile. Post-revolutionary regimes that survive their difficult early years are singularly marked by the choices taken during those formative years. Thus, this study purports only to illuminate what is considered an important period of post-revolutionary Nicaragua.

In keeping with the temporal focus, the argument presented centers on politics within Nicaragua. The new regime initially enjoyed widespread foreign support. Foreign assistance came from numerous countries, ranging from Bulgaria to Mexico to the United States. Nicaragua's foreign debt was renegotiated on terms unprecedented in their generosity, offering a grace period on both interest and principal. Yet even in this favorable international environment, the new regime got caught in a web of economic difficulties.

To be sure, from the onset, the new Nicaraguan regime was confronted with armed resistance. Although resistance was initially isolated and poorly organized, U.S. assistance to the remnants of Somoza's national guard who had fled to Honduras and the concurrent cooperation of Honduras have resulted in a well-organized and well-financed counterrevolution. This locus of resistance has been augmented by disgruntled Miskito Indians and by the opening of a second front along the Costa Rican border by the legendary Eden Pastora. Fighting began in earnest in December 1982 and has continued unabated.

The areas in which fighting has taken place are relatively marginal to the economy. The bulk of the GNP is generated in the Pacific region, which has been free from fighting. The most consequential material cost of the counterrevolution to the new regime has been the opportunity cost of devoting attention and resources to the struggle to defeat the counterrevolutionaries, a cost that is reaching staggering proportions. In 1984, for example, defense officially absorbed 25 percent of government expenditures, but actual costs were probably even higher. Understanding the multifaceted costs to the revolutionary regime inflicted by the counterrevolution will be important in explaining the continued course of Nicaragua, but the counterrevolution was not important in the first three years of the revolution and hence is not discussed here.

The argument advanced suggests that the counterrevolution and U.S. aggression have aggravated economic difficulties and political contradictions and that they retard, if not stymie, efforts at redressing these problems. Others, including some who are more than just apologists for the FSLN, will predictably reverse the order of explanation. The evidence presented here refutes that facile approach. In a broader sense, this study joins the work of others in arguing that to understand the patterns of change in developing nations, more attention should be paid to the capacity for autonomous choice on the part of local actors, both private and public. Such an approach should avoid being state-centric. While the state is often the dominant actor in developing polities, there are many actors with different resources and ambitions. Indeed, the key to understanding political change can reside with seemingly innocuous socioeconomic groups, who are important for what they do not do as well as for what they do.

Chapter 1 draws on the experience of similarly situated post-revolutionary regimes to present a theoretical explanation of the structural constraints on post-revolutionary regimes and how they inevitably complicate efforts to achieve radical change. This book seeks to be both theoretical and empirical, the assumption being that the pungency of theory is best demonstrated in the specificity of analysis. Nicaragua's experience has been consistent with the theoretical model presented. Understanding the Nicaraguan case is useful because the new regime's relative openness allows further clarification of the possibilities and problems of radical and social change in small developing countries. Chapter 2 discusses the regime's consolidation of power and its articulation of policy goals. Chapters 3 through 6 analyze the dialectical relationship between state initiatives and society's reaction to them.

This work emphasizes Nicaragua's rural economy. Barring the outbreak of internecine conflict in Central America, the greatest challenge to the Nicaraguan Revolution lies in rural Nicaragua. As in most developing countries, the most severe poverty in Nicaragua has always been in the rural areas. Somewhat paradoxically, the rural areas of the country are also the source of the nation's wealth: 80 percent of the foreign exchange, so necessary to a small state like Nicaragua, is derived from agriculture. Around 70 percent of the population earns its living from the land. Meeting the promises of the revolution depends on the performance of the agricultural sector. Agriculture not only provides employment, income, and the foreign exchange necessary for maintaining consumption, but it is also the base for generating capital essential for investment.

Mode of Inquiry

Given the importance of agriculture in Nicaragua and the poverty in rural areas, much can be learned about revolutionary change in small developing countries by observing how the new Nicaraguan regime has responded to the challenges and exigencies posed by various strata in the agricultural sector and how these strata have in turn responded to state policies and programs. The approach adopted here is sector analysis, with four representative sectors studied in depth:

1. Cotton producers. Until recently, cotton was the most dynamic sector of the economy and the largest generator of foreign exchange. Nearly all cotton is grown on large estates using an advanced level of technology.

2. Coffee producers. In Nicaragua, coffee is grown largely by small holders using a low or intermediate level of technology. However, there are also large producers.

3. Basic grain producers. Maize, beans, rice, and sorghum are grown principally by peasants using a low level of technology.

4. Wage laborers. The rural economy of Nicaragua does not offer stable employment to a large percentage of rural Nicaraguans, but it does provide many Nicaraguans seasonal employment in the harvests of coffee, cotton, and sugar.

These sectors provide a cross section not only of different agricultural strata but also of different social classes. At the same time, there are important class differences within each of the sectors, and these provide both illuminating insights and a certain amount of control to test variables other than class. For example, the presence or absence of differences between the fates of poor and wealthy coffee producers can help us draw inferences about the relative importance of class status. There are obvious linkages between the four sectors, and an effort is made to understand their symbiotic relationships.

The market provides the locus for analyzing various strata of rural Nicaragua. Through intervention in the market, the state seeks to manipulate the fortunes and behavior of specific economic groups and, more generally, of classes. In brief, the state structures the pattern of advantage both within the countryside and between town and country—principally through the distribution of resources and the regulation of prices. Government intervention in markets is inherently political; market intervention generates political resources, which are distributed to build organized support for political elites and their policies. For their part, rural dwellers use the market to extract concessions from the state or simply as a defense against it.

Sector analysis allows for more specificity and depth than would emerge from a broader or more general treatment. Taken together, the analyses of different sectors provide a firm empirical foundation for examining how the state has interacted with different classes. Sector analysis is also inescapably comparative; it allows for a comparison of similarities and differences between sectors that is heuristically and theoretically useful. However, sector analysis is not necessarily inclusive; important variables or actors may be left out. But a cursory survey of other Nicaraguan economic strata, including the incipient industrial sector and the large informal urban sector, suggests that the view that emerges here is representative of Nicaragua.

Sources of Data

The difficulties of conducting research in a post-revolutionary developing country did not permit some of the more standard methods of data collection for this study. Because many of the data sources were not as systematic as desired, every effort was made to use multiple sources when possible. Field research was carried out between September 1981 and August 1982 and between June and August 1983. A two-week visit to Nicaragua was made in January 1984. Most of the information used in the analysis came from the following sources:

1. published information, ranging from government documents to newspaper articles;
2. the work of nongovernmental organizations, principally the Union of Nicaraguan Agricultural Producers (UPANIC), the Central American Institute of Business Administration (INCAE), and the Institute for Economic and Social Research (INIES);
3. unpublished government documents from the Ministry of Agriculture and Agrarian Reform (MIDINRA), the Center for the Study of Agrarian Reform (CIERA), the Ministry of Planning (MIPLAN), the National Development Bank, and to a lesser extent, the Central Bank;
4. open-ended interviews with rural laborers, agricultural producers, and government officials working in various capacities on the problems of rural Nicaragua.

Because of conflicting views and data, the use of multiple data sources was essential in overcoming problems of reliability.

Statistics on agricultural production presented numerous difficulties. Different government ministries often have conflicting statistics. Occasionally, even offices within the same ministry have conflicting statistics. Discrepancies between statistics presented in published government reports and those presented in internal government documents suggest that at least occasionally statistics are manipulated for political purposes. Government officials who made internal government documents available maintained that the statistics they contained were more reliable than published reports. For the most part, statistics used in this study are from a combination of nongovernment sources and internal government documents. The Nicaraguan Central Bank has traditionally had the most reliable statistics, and an effort was made to verify statistics used here with knowledgeable officials of the Central Bank.

Approximately two hundred subsistence farmers and/or wage laborers were interviewed during a ten-month period. Because they move between subsistence farming and wage labor, poor rural Nicaraguans cannot be described as belonging in one sector or the other. The most detailed interviews with subsistence farmers (who produce mostly basic grains) took place in the departments of León, Carazo, and Chontales. Around fifty coffee growers were interviewed, primarily in the department of Carazo but also in the departments of Managua and Matagalpa. Coffee growers interviewed included those in leadership positions of the coffee growers' association, the National Union of Nicaraguan Coffee Producers (UNCAFENIC). Only about three dozen cotton growers could be interviewed; but they tended to be larger operators, and such a sampling gave a reasonable representation and range of views. Most published and unpublished material obtained was on the cotton sector, compensating for the lower number of interviews. Most of the government officials interviewed were based in Managua, largely because such officials were found to be the best informed and most open. Those interviewed expressed little hesitation about talking frankly in private, although that appeared to be changing in 1983. Of Nicaragua's sixteen departments, twelve were visited.

Individual interviews were supplemented by collaborating on a series of large surveys undertaken by INCAE between 1981 and 1983. A set of surveys was conducted among coffee and cotton producers and among seasonal workers employed in the harvests of the two crops, which together provide well over 50 percent of Nicaragua's foreign-exchange earnings. The largest of the surveys studied rural labor allocation and rural enterprises. For this survey, 503 individuals and personnel from 250 enterprises were interviewed in four Nicaraguan rural communities. These surveys, which were funded by Canada's International Development Research Centre (IDRC), provided a strong empirical base for understanding rural Nicaragua and insights into the complicated relationships that exist among different sectors of the Nicaraguan economy.

1

Third World Revolutionary Regimes

Revolutions are not only significant in themselves, but they also provide an unparalleled opportunity to distinguish the more malleable elements of the social order from its essential components. They allow us to see what changes can be made in a society as well as what changes cannot. In the small, less-developed countries, such as those of Central America, revolution continues to be an important political phenomenon. This is not to suggest that revolutions in such countries are commonplace; they are not. However, they have exploded with enough frequency to be seen as a potential course of action by at least some actors and to have generated wide-ranging debates about their potential accomplishments.

The dimensions of the upheaval and transformations resulting from revolution in this century are boldly stated by America's foremost Marxist theoretician, Paul Sweezy:

> The twentieth century may well go down in history as the century of revolutions. First there was the Russian Revolution, affecting what in territorial terms is by far the largest country in the world. . . . Next came the Chinese Revolution, the culmination of a century-long struggle in the world's most populous country. Other post–World War II revolutions have taken place in Indochina, Korea, Cuba, Portugal's former African colonies, the Horn of Africa, and most recently Southern Yemen, Iran, and Nicaragua. All in all, so far this century, about 30 percent of the earth's land area and 35 percent of its population have

gone through revolutions involving profound structural changes. And all the indications are that the final two decades of the century will witness a continuation and perhaps even an acceleration of this process.[1]

Sweezy is surely correct in forecasting continued revolution. Moreover, he would probably agree that these revolutions can be expected to occur in small, less-developed countries.

Revolution is a fiercely contentious topic. Indeed, there are necessarily ascriptive as well as descriptive components even in identifying a set of events that constitute—or fail to constitute—a revolution.[2] The meaning of revolution is so unclear that Crane Brinton was compelled to begin his monumental book on the subject by stating, "Revolution is one of the looser words."[3] A narrow interpretation would dismiss many self-proclaimed revolutions in the developing world as wars of national liberation. But to the extent that efforts at ending colonial or semicolonial rule result in the assault on established political and economic orders by new and determined political elites, these cases may be considered revolutionary. In any event, the intention here is not to rigidly categorize revolutions (or nonrevolutions) but instead to understand the fate of efforts to achieve abrupt, radical structural change in developing polities. For this purpose, Allende's regime in Chile is as instructive as the Cuban Revolution.

Generalizing about the initial social and political support for revolutions in the developing world is difficult. Where insurrections have been protracted and bitter, such as in Vietnam, a wide spectrum of society has joined in organized and directed struggle. However, in many polities, a traditional low level of political mobilization and participation has enabled revolutionary elites to seize state power without a wide base of support. Ethiopia is a good example. In other cases, mass support was crucial but was spontaneous, sparked perhaps, but not directed, by the actions of a revolutionary vanguard. Even when numerous actors do participate in a revolutionary struggle, they often have conflicting views of ultimate goals. Most actors, particularly

1. Paul M. Sweezy, *Post-Revolutionary Society* (New York: Monthly Review Press, 1980), p. 9.

2. John Dunn, *Modern Revolutions* (Cambridge, England: Cambridge University Press, 1972), p. ix.

3. Crane Brinton, *The Anatomy of Revolution* (New York: Vintage Books, 1965), p. 3.

those from marginal strata of society, fight simply against something, not for something.

Although the initial social bases of support for contemporary revolutions are often narrow, the creation of new political structures to increase, concentrate, and institutionalize power requires revolutionary elites to mobilize support. In carrying out this task, elites confront a number of contradictions and conflicts. On the one hand, assaulting the old order provokes economic disruptions that put potential support groups in economically problematic personal situations. Restoring—and ultimately increasing—economic production and investment to attain greater economic development demands that an investable surplus be accumulated by restricting local groups' consumption.[4] On the other hand, revolutionary leaders often arrive at power with a large debt to their supporters. There may be fervor within the revolutionary movement, but the movement is usually based on mobilization through slogans expressing previously frustrated demands. So the fervor is usually based on anticipation of gratification soon after the insurrection has succeeded. These points of contradiction result in an ongoing tension between political and economic logics.[5]

Like most contradictions, this problem is never neatly resolved. Although the policies and programs implemented in an attempt to address this dilemma are unique for every post-revolutionary polity, there are common characteristics in the social bases of contemporary revolutions. Certain strata can contribute more to economic production than others. Conversely, other strata, such as subsistence farmers, are less important economically. The economically powerful are almost by definition likely to be the target of the revolution; yet their economic power is likely to give them the strongest bargaining position. Similarly, meeting the consumption demands of certain sectors is politically more important than meeting the demands of other sectors. The clearest split is between urban and rural consumers. The ability to generate a crowd in front of the seat of government gives urban dwellers greater power than isolated, marginal peasants; thus, their consumption needs take political precedence. Political bases of support and op-

4. James M. Malloy, "Generation of Political Support and Allocation of Costs," in Carmelo Mesa-Lago, ed., *Revolutionary Change in Cuba* (Pittsburgh: University of Pittsburgh Press, 1971), pp. 26–27.
5. Ibid.

position help explain why post-revolutionary regimes pursue economic policies that—at least initially—exacerbate their difficulties.

Idealism amid Difficulties

Post-revolutionary regimes confront numerous problems. First, there is the material and social damage from the insurrection itself. Second, fledgling regimes face opposition and subversion from defeated political forces and those social strata threatened by post-revolutionary redistribution. Just as Newton demonstrated that every action brings about a reaction, so every revolution evokes a counter-revolution. Reactionary pressure often involves international actors who perceive themselves as threatened by revolutionary change. Resistance to the revolution may be overt, but it is certainly likely also to involve tacit forms of class struggle, such as capital flight and withdrawal from production.

Revolutionary regimes in small Third World countries also face the same constraints as many of their nonrevolutionary counterparts. Material scarcity limits the parameters of innovation. Dependence on exports of one or two primary products and vulnerability to the structure and dynamics of international markets often exist. Politically nascent regimes in countries where national traditions have historically been weak, as in South Yemen and Mozambique, confront social conflict stemming from religious, cultural, tribal, or ethnic schisms. Where national traditions have been strong, as in Vietnam and Korea, the heavy hand of a bureaucratic and authoritarian past weighs on those seeking revolutionary change.[6]

A more consequential set of problems stems from the redistributive policies that post-revolutionary regimes invariably enact. Despite historical, economic, and social differences among contemporary revolutionary regimes in the developing world, there is a rather predictable trajectory. A relatively common set of goals is articulated, which leads to an equally predictable set of initial outcomes. Contemporary revolutions invariably espouse some form of self-defined socialism. Of the principal revolutions of the past century, only the one in Iran has been "conservative." The appeal of socialism to revolutionary elites un-

6. Gordon White, Robin Murray, and Christine White, eds., *Revolutionary Socialist Development in the Third World* (London: Wheatsheaf Books, 1983), pp. 6–7.

doubtedly stems from its anti-imperialist stance and its emphasis on egalitarianism—to be attained by the redistribution of wealth and income. Of course, just what socialism means in practice is widely contested, and socialism in one country can look remarkably different from socialism in another. Still, a study of radical structural change is nearly tantamount to studying efforts toward the "construction of socialism."

Widespread commitment to the ideals of socialism results in a relatively common set of policies:

1. elimination of the economic role of foreign capitalists;
2. state expropriation of large landed estates and industrial enterprises;
3. collectivization of agriculture;
4. state control over the direction of the growth of the economy;
5. income redistribution policies.

An additional shared goal seems to be improving the welfare of lower classes through government services and programs. Examples range from improved health care service to food subsidies.

The two great revolutions of the century—the Russian and the Chinese—have bequeathed Third World countries general guidelines for putting Marx's revolutionary theories into practice. They have suggested not only the previously delineated policy goals, but also organizational and institutional structures. However, small developing countries are distinguished from the Soviet Union and China by their size. The Soviet Union and China are the largest and third largest countries in the world by area (Canada is the second largest). Both the Soviet Union and China pursued autarchic development strategies, possible only because of the enormous resources that each of the two countries possesses. In contrast, small developing countries, defined in relation to their dependence on foreign trade as well as their physical resource base, do not have the necessary resources to pursue an independent development strategy and hence are inescapably tied to world markets. The consequences of this difference are important.

Small revolutionary polities in the developing world do not necessarily have problems different from those of the Soviet Union and China. Indeed, many of the problems appear to be similar. What varies are policy responses generated by their differences in size. The draconian solution of having the state supersede all efforts of the private sector (or, put in a more grisly fashion, of sacrificing the entire old order), is not feasible, except, perhaps, with generous foreign assistance. Dependent on foreign trade, small states cannot swallow the resulting economic disorder and deprivation the way large insular economies can. Equally important, small states are vulnerable to counterrevolutionaries quick to exploit popular discontent. These two vulnerabilities, which are mutually reinforcing, probably explain why so few small developing countries are resolutely Marxist-Leninist.

Constraints on Redistribution

A scrutiny of a number of contemporary post-revolutionary regimes in the Third World suggests that severe structural constraints not only make it difficult for these countries to improve the welfare of lower classes but also promote the adoption of policies directed at other classes, which are inconsistent with revolutionary ideology and rhetoric. Small developing countries need to import, and therefore to export, if they are to maintain consumption levels. If they happen to be blessed with substantial foreign exchange because of mineral wealth or a foreign patron, they have more latitude. But if they are like most developing countries, they will be highly dependent on the production of key sectors that earn foreign exchange—regardless of the ownership of these sectors.

Central government authority is inevitably increased in the aftermath of a revolution.[7] However, while the possibility of state autonomy appears to be enhanced by control of the means of coercion and by a high level of cohesion within the state, autonomy is limited by the state's dependence on resources generated by economic production.[8] This dependence continues even when the state itself controls the means of production in certain economic sectors. The limits of state autonomy become evident as post-revolutionary regimes attempt to promote egalitarianism through redistribution policies.

A principal redistribution strategy is nationalization—confiscated assets are retained and operated by the government on behalf of the

7. Susan Eckstein, *The Impact of Revolution: A Comparative Analysis of Mexico and Bolivia* (Beverly Hills, Calif.: Sage, 1976), p. 40.

8. Nora Hamilton, *The Limits of State Autonomy: Post-Revolutionary Mexico* (Princeton, N.J.: Princeton University Press, 1982), pp. 7–8.

polity. In revolutionary developing countries, the locus of nationalization is usually the sector or sectors that produce foreign exchange. For example, in Bolivia in 1952, the mines were nationalized, as were sugar estates in Cuba in 1959, oil interests in Algeria in 1962, and copper mines in Chile in 1970. Both the way in which the nationalization is carried out and the way in which the nationalized assets are operated have important implications for economic stability and growth.

In most developing countries, the technical and managerial capacity to nationalize all assets does not exist. The lack of feasibility or desirability of the government assuming complete responsibility for economic production leads to the first problem that arises with nationalization: how to carry it out so as not to damage confidence and willingness to invest in what is often the substantial part of the economy remaining in the private sector. The experience of Allende's regime in Chile and of various African states suggests that the private sector is often disinclined to maintain production during attempts at radical structural change for two reasons: (1) loss of short-term financial incentives as a result of government intervention in producers' principal markets and general economic disorder, and (2) uncertainty about future state policies. Both factors are important, but the latter is perhaps more decisive. The uncertainty of the private sector is often well founded; a governing elite may agree on what it would like to achieve but be unsure of precisely how to accomplish goals.[9] The Chilean case suggests that uncertainty is aggravated by the presence in both the public and private sectors of actors arguing for higher bargaining demands, by personal and group animosities, and by a dialectic process in which private sector objectives are due in part to government policies and government policies are conditioned by private sector reactions.[10]

Economic stability and growth also depend on the management of nationalized assets. Public investment will depend critically on the ability of state enterprises to generate a surplus. Because much of the surplus will be invested in the public sector, investment return (that is, the productivity of investment) will depend heavily on the efficiency

9. Antonio Jorge, "Economic Decision-Making in Cuba: The Transition from Capitalism to Communism," *Journal of Interamerican Studies and World Affairs* 25 (May 1983), pp. 251–267.

10. Arturo Valenzuela, *Chile* (Baltimore: Johns Hopkins University Press, 1978), pp. 70 and 77.

of public enterprises. Especially right after nationalization, political pressures are likely to push state enterprises to provide both increased employment and higher wages. For similar noneconomic reasons, state enterprises may be pressured to reduce the selling prices of their goods or services, especially if they are destined for popular consumption.[11] Finally, productivity is likely to be at least initially adversely affected by changes in management staff and ambiguity about management criteria.

The inability of revolutionary regimes to assume complete responsibility for economic activity, uncertainty in the private sector, and difficulties in generating a surplus in nationalized enterprises result in economic turmoil and in declining productivity. Cuba's experience is illuminating. Mesa-Lago describes the immediate effects of efforts to bring about radical change in the Cuban economy:

> The collectivization was too wide and rapid, hence millions of economic microrelations were destroyed at once, breaking the automatic mechanisms of the market when the state was not ready to take over these functions. The new central ministries and agencies lacked coordination among themselves, were hastily organized and staffed with inexperienced personnel, and operated in a freewheeling manner with no control procedures. . . . No investment plan existed; investment decisions were not coordinated but made in an arbitrary manner lacking mechanisms to assure their efficiency; the result was poor capital productivity. Land collectivization . . . dislocated the flow of supplies from the countryside to the towns. Due to lack of information or managerial control, agricultural products badly needed in the cities were lost in the ground or, after being harvested, spoiled because of unavailability of transportation.[12]

The disruption of production has clear and direct consequences for society's welfare, notwithstanding the possible previous usurpation of wealth and income by nonproductive elites.

Just when the economic realities of the supply side indicate real living standards must fall, attempts are made to raise the real living standards of the majority of the people. Large increases in money wages are allocated. The consumption of food and other basic goods is sub-

11. David Morawetz, "Economic Lessons from Some Small Socialist Developing Countries," *World Development* 8 (May-June 1980), pp. 354–355.

12. Carmelo Mesa-Lago, *The Economy of Socialist Cuba: A Two-Decade Appraisal* (Albuquerque: University of New Mexico Press, 1981), p. 16.

sidized. The provision of social services is upgraded and expanded. Employment generation schemes are launched. In addition, labor takes its "historical vacation," seeking to lessen the commitment and burden of employment. For example, after the Cuban Revolution, hours worked by agricultural laborers fell from eight to an average of four and a half to five per day.[13]

Efforts to redistribute wealth and income to those who constitute the large stratum of the poor are handicapped by the fact that these individuals are marginal to the rest of the economy. Raising the productivity of populations that lack so many of the productive requisites, such as minimum investment capital, education, and skills, is difficult.[14] Thus, redistributed resources are invested, but with little yield, or simply consumed. The beneficiaries of redistribution policies may regard their gains as the spoils of victory and not as capital to be prudently husbanded. The rhetoric of the revolutionary elite often fosters such an attitude.

The more militant the revolution, the more likely it is to get caught between falls in economic output and ignited expectations and the ensuing necessity of either compromising itself or permitting the economy to fall to politically dangerous levels. Industrialization and modernization have made this increasingly the case, particularly in situations where elites "produce" as well as "consume." The stereotypical nineteenth-century absentee landlord has more often than not been replaced by the competent farmer employing modern agricultural inputs and practices. While ruling elites still monopolize a disproportionate share of wealth and income in nearly all developing countries, destroying them as a class is certainly more costly than if they had been a traditional idle elite.

As laudable as the intentions of post-revolutionary regimes may be, their policies tend to produce severe economic problems that undermine the welfare of their citizens. There appears to be a classic pattern in the immediate post-revolutionary period of small Third World countries. One set of policies leads to dislocations in productive sectors, resulting in a reduced national output. This decrease in production is often concentrated in the more remunerative export sector because it

13. Ibid., p. 125; Arthur MacEwan, *Revolution and Economic Development in Cuba* (New York: St. Martin's Press, 1981), p. 145.
14. William Ascher, *Scheming for the Poor* (Cambridge: Harvard University Press, 1984), p. 34.

tends to have been monopolized by elites (precisely because it was more remunerative).

A complementary set of policies designed to aid impoverished sectors absorbs large amounts of resources without a corresponding rise in output—at least in the short run—because the resources are principally used for consumption and not investment. Together the two sets of policies produce an economic crisis. In short, "supply" decreases and "demand" increases. Given the dependence of small developing countries on international trade, the locus of the crisis is usually the balance of payments and the availability of foreign exchange. Drawing down reserves and accepting foreign assistance and borrowing can help cover the resulting imbalance, but ultimately they are likely to prove insufficient.

The case of Allende's regime in Chile illustrates the severity of the economic crisis in which post-revolutionary regimes can find themselves. Morawetz describes its difficulties:

> Despite an initial increase in nominal wages of 50 percent in 1971, and several even greater increases during the next 2 years, by the time the Allende government was overthrown Chilean wages were 25–50 percent lower in real terms than they had been in 1970. The rate of inflation increased from 18 to 33 percent in 1965–1970 to over 400 percent in 1973; the budget deficit of the central government rose from less than 1.5 percent of GDP in 1968–1970 to 8–9 percent of GDP in 1971–1972 and by a further 9 percent in 1972–1973. A survey conducted in a popular chain of co-operative stores late in 1972 showed that out of a range of 3,000 basic household products that were normally stocked, more than 2,500 were unavailable. Rationing was introduced early in 1973. The ratio of net agricultural imports to total exports rose from an average of 18 percent in 1965–1970 to nearly 60 percent in 1972. The balance-of-payments deficit on current account increased from $104 million in 1970 to more than $500 million in 1972. And foreign reserves, which had stood at over $350 million when Allende took office, had fallen to below zero within 2 years.[15]

Chile's experience is not unique. For example, the Bolivian Revolution of 1952 resulted in a price level rise from 100 in 1951 to 2,816 in 1956.[16]

15. Morawetz, "Economic Lessons," pp. 357–358.
16. Walter Gomez, "Bolivia: Problems of a Pre- and Post-Revolutionary Export Economy," *Journal of Developing Areas* 10 (July 1976), p. 477.

Crisis Economics

An examination of a number of contemporary post-revolutionary regimes suggests that there are predictable state responses to the inevitable financial crisis. The nature of the post-revolutionary crisis is inherently inflationary—expansionary fiscal policies (and undoubtedly expansionary monetary policies as well) coupled with falling production of essential goods and services. There is likely to be an equally serious balance-of-payment deficit, precipitated mostly by reduced exports but perhaps also by increased imports.[17] Too much money chasing too few goods ordinarily results in inflation. In order to forestall inflation and protect the purchasing power of the lower classes, especially urban residents, regimes are likely to institute price controls. An example is post-revolutionary Ethiopia's commercial policies: "The Derg was determined to impose controls on food staples in order to curb inflation—a major cause of the civilian agitation in February 1974—and to reduce the risk of further discontent in urban areas."[18] Of course, controlling prices of consumer goods in a period of generally rising prices hurts producers, who are likely to be experiencing at least some rising costs. Revolutionary regimes are likely to slight producers in order to aid consumers. What begins as hostility toward wealthy producers and a commitment to improving the consumption of the poor slowly becomes a generalized bias against the producer and for the consumer.

The government may be all the more disposed to control prices of domestically produced goods if imported goods are increasing in price, which is likely if there is a large deficit in the balance of payments. In effect, the government may try to control prices where it can. However, low prices can be a disincentive to increasing production or even to maintaining existing levels of production. Price disincentives may even offset specific government policies designed to stimulate production. Although certain sectors may benefit from controlled prices in the short run, ultimately all sectors of the economy, and the polity at large, may suffer if there is a resulting decline in output. If

17. Morawetz, "Economic Lessons," pp. 358–360.
18. Marina Ottaway and David Ottaway, *Ethiopia* (New York: Africana Publishing Company, 1978), p. 65.

this policy is taken too far, Mao's statement about the Soviet experience, "draining the pond to catch the fish," may apply.

Although from an economic point of view the new regime's price controls are not prudent, there are political reasons that explain—but do not necessarily justify—the policies. The first is ideological; production for private gain is not held in high esteem. The second is simple expediency. Price controls do provide some short-term relief, and regimes under pressure often do not have the political "resources" to think beyond the short term. Finally, there is urban bias. Urban dwellers are always more visible and politically more powerful than rural dwellers. Appeasing urban constituents is important, and low prices, especially for food, are a convenient policy instrument. Of course, governments are usually aware of the economic costs incurred by a lack of incentives to producers. Governments may, on occasion, raise producer prices in well-publicized attempts to offer incentives, but producers are likely always to be belatedly trying to catch up with rising production costs.

Post-revolutionary regimes are also likely to allocate state resources in a way that is inconsistent with revolutionary rhetoric. The necessity of maintaining production prompts post-revolutionary regimes to allocate state resources where they can be most productive, and not where they are most needed. Thus, in the aftermath of the Algerian Revolution, state efforts centered on further developing the hydrocarbon industry to the neglect of the populous and impoverished agricultural sector.[19] Mozambique provides an even more revealing example. Pressure to increase food production has led the government to allocate considerable funding to the state farms formerly owned by the Portuguese settler population. This policy is perceived as being the easiest and quickest way to increase production. Concomitantly, communal villages, where the bulk of the rural populace lives and where poverty is most acute, have received few resources.[20] A contradiction has emerged between the goals of improving the welfare of rural vil-

19. Arthur Banks, *Economic Handbook of the World: 1981* (New York: McGraw-Hill, 1981), pp. 31–32.
20. James H. Mittleman, "The Dialectic of National Autonomy and Global Participation: Alternatives to Conventional Strategies of Development—Mozambique Experience," *Alternatives* 5 (November 1979), p. 313; Allen Isaacman and Barbara Isaacman, *Mozambique* (Boulder, Colo.: Westview Press, 1983), p. 157.

lagers and increasing food production. Because the rural poor contribute only marginally to the national economy, especially in foreign-exchange generation, they tend to be the most neglected when the state allocates resources, despite claims to the contrary.

In the post-revolutionary era, drawing a simple dichotomy between the "state" and "private" sectors is likely to prove impossible, although, of course, there are obvious differences between the two. The state has such a wide range of policy instruments at its command that it decisively influences the private sector. Most of these policy instruments entail intervention in the major markets for the products affecting producers—the markets for the products they consume and sell and for land, labor, and capital. Government pricing decisions can condition the extent to which producers maintain output and investment as much as such bold policies as nationalization decrees.

As post-revolutionary regimes confront an inevitable deficit in their balance of payments, they are likely to offer concessions, such as the price of output, to increase production. These concessions are likely to be made to those with economic strength and not the reverse, as revolutionary rhetoric would suggest. Furthermore, states—or at least bureaucracies within states—are fully capable of putting their narrow self-interest above the welfare of weaker strata of society. Government assistance and prices for producers are likely to depend not on their class status but on (1) the importance of the output to the national economy, and (2) the elasticity of supply.

The granting of concessions to productive strata is likely to be contradictory, resulting in mixed signals to economic actors and confusion over the "rules of the game." Because concessions run counter to revolutionary programs, one set of policies offers incentives and another set, disincentives. There is a danger that differentiated concessions will invite government corruption, as happened in Bolivia when the revolutionary regime of 1952 offered variable access to foreign exchange.[21] More important, economic concessions are often manipulated for political purposes with little regard for economic costs. For example, although price policies with clear incentives are the most effective way of increasing food production, governments prefer to in-

21. Gomez, "Bolivia," pp. 474–475.

vest in projects where the state can more easily exact allegiance from beneficiaries.[22] Thus, the net result of concessions offered to stimulate declining production is likely to be still further economic disorder.

Conflicting interests can also exist between those marginal sectors that the revolutionary regime proclaims itself committed to aid. All governments seek to maintain "solvency," and that imposes a need to maintain production, garner resources such as foreign exchange, and keep consumption on a par with available goods and services. Rhetoric notwithstanding, the proclivity is always to fulfill these needs through the simplest means available.

The contradictory nature of policies pursued by regimes committed to radical structural change can be illustrated by the fate of attempts at agrarian reform. Despite high aspirations, agrarian reforms seem to fall prey to inconspicuous government fiscal and monetary policies that offset the government's more conspicuous distribution of land. During the 1970s, Peru launched an ambitious agrarian reform that by 1978 broke the power of the rural oligarchy in the traditional Andean estates and coastal plantations. However, during the very period in which the regime tried to satisfy the peasants' most basic demand by giving them land, government import and price policies were consistently biased against the agricultural producer. Pricing problems and macroeconomic problems left the peasantry in poverty, and agricultural output failed to keep pace even with population growth.[23] A similar outcome has been reported in Mozambique.[24] Perhaps the most extreme case has been Algeria, where the government faced the problem of finding potential recipients because of serious agricultural price disincentives.[25] Whereas agrarian reforms in the absence of revolution are likely to be thwarted by entrenched elites, revolutionary agrarian reform is likely to be offset by the economic disruptions inherent in

22. Robert H. Bates, *Markets and States in Tropical Africa: The Political Basis of Agricultural Policies* (Berkeley and Los Angeles: University of California Press, 1981), p. 5.
23. Howard Handelman, "Peasants, Landlords and Bureaucrats: The Politics of Agrarian Reform in Peru," in Howard Handelman, ed., *The Politics of Agrarian Change in Asia and Latin America* (Bloomington: Indiana University Press, 1981), p. 119.
24. Mittleman, "The Dialectic," p. 8.
25. Keith Sutton, "The Progress of Algeria's Agrarian Reform and Its Settlement Implications," *The Maghreb Review* 3 (January-April 1978), p. 10.

any revolution and by the political inability of revolutionary leadership to put the needs of marginal rural peasants over more powerful and well-endowed actors when the state is in the midst of economic difficulties.

Conclusions

In the post-revolutionary era, the deterioration of the economy is likely to be so extensive, and the reactivation of the economy so difficult, that the promised "liberation" of peasants and laborers is not forthcoming. Instead, peasants suffer from low prices as the new regime hastily tries to protect urban consumers and from neglect as the state concentrates on managing large state farms that are judged more important for the reactivation of the economy. Laborers suffer from an enforced policy of "austerity and efficiency" that demands continued sacrifices. This state of affairs results not because revolutionary leaders desire it; they would doubtless like to provide a better life for the poor. Rather, the exigencies of the situation make the continued impoverishment of peasants and laborers a structural necessity.

Legitimacy for a revolution depends on political issues; legitimacy for a post-revolutionary regime depends on economic performance. Hence, a revolutionary regime must take care not to undermine the welfare of those sectors that it is committed to assist. This caution is especially important if a revolutionary regime is threatened by a counterrevolution; if lower classes become dissatisfied and cynical, counterrevolutionaries—domestic or international—may be able to garner strength that they otherwise could not hope to gain. This has clearly happened recently in Mozambique. It is a truism of both revolutionary and counterrevolutionary insurgency that success depends on generating some popular support or at least the tacit support of those disaffected with the existing regime.

The inability of contemporary post-revolutionary regimes to provide much in the way of material improvements to their citizens does not necessarily mean that the revolutions should not have been carried out. Just as Marx wrote that the French Revolution cleared away lots of "medieval rubbish," so have recent revolutions in the developing countries cleared away colonial or neocolonial relics. These relics are not only despotic and unjust, but often are also obstacles to broad-based development. However, post-revolutionary regimes are—at least in the short run—unlikely to deliver on the economic promises they make. Indeed, the trajectory of post-revolutionary regimes presented here suggests that these countries are likely to fall into an economic morass, or as Morawetz put it, "a first class economic mess."[26]

Leadership is important in post-revolutionary regimes, and there is a marked difference between such revolutionary leaders as Amílcar Cabral (Guinea-Bissau) and Forbes Burnham (Guyana). Still, the uniformities of contemporary post-revolutionary regimes in small developing countries suggest that the parameters of choice are limited. Predictable decisions are thrust on revolutionary elites by circumstances beyond their control. Thus, the effect of leadership on events seems to be of degree (and perhaps sequence) and not of kind. Given the vulnerability of post-revolutionary regimes (for example, Bolivia in 1956), these incremental differences can be decisive.

Overcoming the constraints of post-revolutionary rule seems to depend on the new regime recognizing that the period immediately after the revolution is not going to be a time of rising living standards and conveying this message to its followers. First, the regime thus has to deflate expectations that it raised in the insurrection period without losing its legitimacy in the process. Second, the regime must be resolutely clear about the parameters of public and private economic activity so as to avoid the desertion of the entire private sector. Third, efforts need to be made to increase productivity and output. This increase can be accomplished in part by redistributing poorly exploited assets, but more important is promoting efficiency, innovation, and investment. Although this task is slow, difficult, and costly, there is no alternative.

26. Morawetz, "Economic Lessons," p. 361.

2

The New Nicaraguan State

THE NICARAGUAN Revolution faces many threats and challenges. The government that has replaced the Somoza dynasty is based on a coalition of classes that is held together only tenuously and is confronted by counterrevolutionaries at home and abroad. It even faces the danger of being dragged into international conflict. Although these political factors are important and receive a great deal of attention, barring a major outbreak of internecine conflict in Central America, the Nicaraguan Revolution will probably stand or fall on the performance of the agricultural sector.

Around 70 percent of the population earn their living from the land, and agriculture provides more than 80 percent of Nicaragua's exports.[1] After all the speeches have been made and all the government proclamations have been decreed, it will still be the availability of food, housing, and work that will determine the popular support for the government. What counts now is not the promises that are made, but the promises that are kept. In Nicaragua, meeting the promises of the revolution depends crucially on the performance of the agricultural sector.

In order to understand the development of the Nicaraguan economy, its problems and its potential, three facets of Nicaragua must be considered: its resources, its historical development, and the revolution and

1. *Latin American Weekly Report*, 22 August 1980.

the new regime's policies. These topics overlap, but they can be discussed separately.

The historical development of Nicaragua has led to a dependence on the agricultural sector that cannot be rapidly alleviated. Equally important, attempting any structural change of the agricultural sector has a significant cost—at least in the short run. More specifically, the historical development of Nicaragua has resulted in heavy dependence on agroexports. The new government is committed to helping the peasantry, but doing so can easily hurt the agroexport sector. Because Nicaragua desperately needs the export earnings, the central task in the agricultural sector is to simultaneously improve the welfare of the peasantry and maintain the strength of the agroexport sector.

Nicaragua's Resources

Nicaragua is the largest and least densely populated of the Central American states. The country lies entirely within the tropics; it borders Costa Rica in the south and Honduras in the north and extends from the Caribbean to the Pacific. Although the republic is only about the size of Wisconsin, it is a country of geographic contrast. The mountainous Central American cordillera rises to a modest height in the western third of the country, running northwest to southeast, and contains eighteen volcanoes. In the east, the country slopes toward the Caribbean, ending in the once-notorious Miskito coast, an aptly named jungle area that once provided refuge for Caribbean buccaneers. One of the peculiar geographic features of the country is the presence of the Nicaragua and Managua lakes—the two largest lakes south of Texas. They are linked by the Tipitapa River and form part of an underdeveloped transport system.[2]

Because of its geographic diversity, Nicaragua is commonly divided into four main regions. The *western plains* of the Pacific coast are volcanic plains ranging from sea level to an elevation of several hundred feet with rainy and dry seasons of approximately six months each. The rainy season usually begins in May and normally ends in October. There is considerable variation in the rainfall within the re-

2. John Martz, *Central America* (Chapel Hill: University of North Carolina Press, 1959); World Bank, *The Economic Development of Nicaragua* (Baltimore: Johns Hopkins University Press, 1959), p. xxiii; M. Monteforte, *Centro America* (Mexico City: Universidad Nacional Autónoma de México, 1972), pp. 31–32.

gion: the mean is forty-five inches, but the range is from sixteen to seventy inches. The volcanic ash soils are of high fertility.

The *Managua-Carazo uplands* (sierras) are a comparatively small sierra and upland plateau ranging in height from about thirteen hundred to four thousand feet. The climate is cooler and somewhat more humid than that of the western plains region, as might be expected from the elevation.

The *central mountain region* (Matagalpa-Jinotega) is situated in the range of mountains forming the Continental Divide, with an elevation ranging from fifteen hundred to about fifty-five hundred feet. The topography is for the most part rugged, though there are lowland valleys and plateaus. The climate is cool, with little seasonal change but marked diurnal change. On the whole, the soil is not quite as fertile as in other regions. The vegetation consists of, at least in the higher portions of the region, a tropical forest climate, mixed in species. At lower elevations, fire and agricultural activities have considerably damaged these forests, and much of the land is in the successional stages of secondary grassland and tree-and-grass savanna.

The *eastern plains* of the Atlantic coast are low lying, low relief, hot, and humid. Rain is heavier than elsewhere in the country, with the rainy season extending over nine to twelve months of the year. Annual rainfall of over one hundred fifty inches is not uncommon. There is a wide range of soils. The prevailing vegetation is tropical evergreen hardwood forest of mixed composition; the northeast has an extensive area of pine flats. These forests are estimated to cover nearly twenty million acres, of which about one-quarter is believed to be commercially valuable. Mineral deposits, especially gold ore, are potentially significant, though largely undeveloped.

Despite its geographic diversity and richness, Nicaragua has the smallest population of any Central American country. One of the first tasks of the new government was to conduct a census. The population was put at roughly three million—nearly a million more than was previously thought. The inhabitants are largely mestizo, predominantly Indian but with an admixture of European, mainly Spanish, blood. Probably some 75 percent are mestizo, another 10 percent white or predominantly white, and the remainder Indians, blacks, zambos, or mulattoes. Members of the latter group live, for the most part, on the east coast.

The population is highly concentrated. About 60 percent of all the inhabitants live in a narrow belt along the Pacific, two hundred miles long but only twelve to sixty miles wide. A second belt, averaging sixty miles farther inland, contains another 32 percent of the population. The eastern plains region, which contains more than half the total land area, contains only 8 percent of the population. Despite the concentration of the population, overall density is a little over half that of Costa Rica and perhaps a fifth that of El Salvador. A high percentage of arable land is not in cultivation. This factor, among others, indicates both the degree of underdevelopment and the potential of the country.[3]

When the bountiful natural resources of Nicaragua—the temperate climate of much of the country, the fertile volcanic soil, the ready availability of water, and the lush forest that covers over half the country— are added to the favorable human-land ratio, it becomes evident that Nicaragua has great potential for economic development. To be sure, the geographic contrasts of the country do present some problems. This is especially true for the eastern part of the country, which is very tropical and which, in addition, contains a population that differs ethnically from that of other regions. The country is rich in resources, but its people are, on the average, poor. In fact, it has been written that "until recent years, probably no Central American state was wasting its potential as shamelessly as Nicaragua."[4] Understanding why the potential of Nicaragua has not been developed necessitates studying its history, particularly that of the rural sector because agriculture has always been the mainstay of the economy.

Historical Development of Nicaragua

Although Spain's control of Central America was never as pervasive as is commonly believed, it did have an enormous impact on the Central American countries. Because of the Spanish feudal traditions, industrial backwardness, and trade policy, agriculture predominated on the isthmus, and social and economic security and advancement in the colony depended on landholding and control of labor to work the land.[5] Furthermore, Spanish colonialism contributed at least

3. Monteforte, *Centro America*, pp. xxiii–xxv.
4. Martz, *Central America*, p. 165.
5. Ralph Woodward, Jr., *Central America* (New York: Oxford University Press, 1976), p. 42.

indirectly to the creation of large estates devoted to the production of export crops.

Even during the colonial centuries, the pattern of monoculture, with all its weaknesses, characterized the economic system of Central America. This pattern included dependence on food imports while the hacienda—the key to the economic and social structure of colonial life—devoted its entire effort to producing cacao, indigo, cattle, and other export crops; erratic fluctuations of world prices and competition from other sources of supply; the domestic debtor-creditor relationship; the reliance on outside capital; and the chronic need for cheap transportation facilities.[6] To be sure, during the colonial period, most of the inhabitants of Central America from Chiapas to Costa Rica were engaged in simple subsistence agriculture or in producing foodstuffs for local markets. Small farms and large estates alike produced corn, livestock, beans, and other vegetables and fruits for domestic consumption. However, the economic well-being of the isthmus has always rested on the production of export commodities.

As was the case in most Central American countries, the production of cacao was the first important source of wealth for Nicaraguan landowners. However, competition from areas bordering on the Caribbean, closer to the European market, eventually destroyed that lucrative trade. Nicaragua subsequently concentrated on raising livestock, selling meat and by-products to El Salvador and western Guatemala. The growth of the European textile industry and the accompanying demand for colorful dyes gave Nicaragua, and Central America in general, an opportunity to recover some of the ground lost in the cacao decline. Guatemala produced a large quantity of cochineal, and Guatemala and El Salvador became major exporters of indigo. Nicaragua produced less indigo but along with Honduras was able to increase its exports of meat and foodstuffs to Guatemala and El Salvador because agriculture there was dominated by the production of cochineal and indigo.[7]

The reforms and policies of politicians bent on material progress, coupled with the industrial transformation of Western Europe and the United States, which created an almost insatiable demand for raw materials during the second half of the nineteenth century, helped fix the

6. Mario Rodríguez, *Central America* (Englewood Cliffs, N.J.: Prentice-Hall, 1965), p. 52.
7. Woodward, *Central America*, p. 70; Rodríguez, *Central America*, pp. 53–54.

stamp of monoculture on Central America's economy. New products replaced cochineal and indigo, which by the end of the 1850s could no longer compete with Europe's chemical dyes. Coffee and bananas became the major foreign-exchange earners. Because they required large outlays of capital and provided a high rate of return, landholdings became increasingly concentrated into large plantations owned by foreign corporations and enterprising Central American families.

The heavy emphasis on large-scale, export-oriented agriculture had three important consequences besides increased concentration of land:

1. The social patterns of the past were perpetuated in a more demanding and impersonal form.

2. As dependence of the Central American states on overseas areas grew, trade among them was not fostered, and they had little or no economic relations with each other.

3. The role of foreigners increased dramatically.

Of course, all these consequences of large-scale, export-oriented agriculture are interrelated and complementary.[8]

The development of large-scale, export-oriented agriculture with its attendant economic and social consequences was as pervasive in Nicaragua as elsewhere in Central America. Although coffee was not cultivated in Nicaragua as early as in most other Central American countries, by the 1870s it was an important crop. Its emergence as a major export crop was accompanied by increased concentration of land, accentuated class differences, and increased importance of foreigners and foreign trade in the economy.[9] Germans, Frenchmen, and North Americans together produced more coffee than the Nicaraguan producers.[10] In addition, foreigners led the way in the technology of cultivating, processing, and, most important, marketing coffee in Europe and North America.

The Atlantic coast of Nicaragua was long coveted by Great Britain

8. Rodríguez, *Central America*, p. 102; R. Menjívar, "Los Problemas del Mundo Rural," in E. Torres-Rivas et al., eds., *Centroamérica: Hoy* (Mexico City: Siglo Veintiuno Editores, 1975), pp. 272–273; Woodward, *Central America*, p. 132.

9. Jaime Wheelock, *Imperialismo y Dictadura* (Mexico City: Siglo Veintiuno Editores, 1979), pp. 13–21. For an excellent discussion of the impact of coffee production on Costa Rica, a country supposedly of yeoman farmers, see Mitchell Seligson, *Peasants of Costa Rica and the Development of Agrarian Capitalism* (Madison: University of Wisconsin Press, 1980).

10. Woodward, *Central America*, p. 157.

in defiance of Spain, and Britain actively traded with the indigenous people (principally Miskito Indians) and the more recent settlers of the area. Great Britain gave up its territorial aspirations for the coast in 1860, but trade and investment continued.[11] American companies subsequently joined British companies in the pursuit of lumber, gold, and rubber. Later the United States Fruit Company began producing bananas for export in the hitherto unproductive lowlands of the coast.[12] Gold and banana production developed some importance. However, given the enclave nature of gold and banana production, accentuated by the geographic and ethnic differences between the Pacific and Atlantic coasts, coffee was the only product that generated both growth in the national economy and local wealth. Coffee came to be the most important earner of foreign exchange, and its cultivation provided significant employment.

The economies of Central America, which began to buckle in the 1890s, were further weakened by the downswing of coffee prices before World War I. Bananas and other commodities took up the slack somewhat but never enough to put the countries on a firm footing. All the Central American states rapidly became heavily indebted to foreign creditors. In fact, at one point, service on the national debt was the major item in the budgets of every Central American state. Nicaragua's debt problem, in combination with opposition to the nationalistic dictator José Santos Zelaya, prompted United States intervention in Nicaragua that eventually resulted in a military occupation that was to last until 1933 and in the establishment of a puppet regime.[13]

The dislocations in world trade during World War I further increased the dependence of Nicaragua (and of all other Central American countries) on the United States as a market and as a source of credit. As long as prosperity reigned in the north, financial assistance from the United States tended to cover superficially the weaknesses of the Nicaraguan economy. The crash of 1929 had a disastrous impact, however. Coffee prices plummeted to new lows, and loans were suddenly not available. It took World War II, with its demand for products

11. Ibid., p. 131; Rodríguez, *Central America*, p. 103.

12. Philip A. Dennis, "The Costeños and the Revolution in Nicaragua," *Journal of Interamerican Studies and World Affairs* 23 (August 1981), pp. 280–281.

13. Woodward, *Central America*, pp. 194–195; Rodríguez, *Central America*, p. 126.

the Axis powers controlled in the Far East, to revitalize and diversify the Nicaraguan economy.[14]

Nicaragua is said to have enjoyed an economic renaissance in the aftermath of World War II, developing the most flourishing economy in Central America in the 1950s. The dictator General Anastacio Somoza, who ruled from 1936 to 1956, is credited with much of the growth in Nicaragua's economy, although his economic record could not have been possible without Nicaragua's bountiful resources and fertile land. Somoza purposefully developed those assets and began work on such prerequisites for national development as a road system, port facilities, public health, schools, a labor code, and social security. He demonstrated an awareness of the weakness inherent in monoculture and strove to balance the economy by encouraging agricultural diversification. Somoza's developmental policies were continued by his two sons after the dictator was assassinated in 1956. The elder of Somoza's sons, Luís, succeeded his father but succumbed to a heart attack in 1967, leaving Anastacio, Jr., as ruler of the nation.

The Somozas benefited most from Nicaragua's growth. Indeed, this family dynasty was the strongest and most durable in Latin American history. They acquired huge tracts of land and vast financial resources, which were invested in industry, mining, and commerce both in Nicaragua and abroad, while the majority of the population lived in poverty. After the revolution, it was learned that the Somozas and their associates owned over 25 percent of the agricultural land in the country and 147 commercial entities, ranging from the Mercedes Benz dealership to a cement factory. This economic control enabled the Somozas to eliminate serious competition and neutralize most opposition while they pointed to statistical gains in Nicaraguan production and per capita income.[15] Opposition that could not be bought off was ruthlessly crushed.[16]

Philip Warnken's careful analysis demonstrates both the dominance of the export sector under the Somozas and the relative poverty of most rural Nicaraguans. Drawing on data from the national census and the

14. Rodríguez, *Central America*, pp. 126–127.
15. Woodward, *Central America*, pp. 220–221.
16. The ruthlessness of the Somoza regime is described in Amnesty International, *The Republic of Nicaragua: An Amnesty International Report* (USA: Amnesty International Publications, 1977).

Central Bank of Nicaragua, he shows that although more than five times the number of farms produced basic grain crops in 1971 as produced export crops (coffee, cotton, and sugar), export crops accounted for 49 percent of the total value of production, whereas food crops (maize, beans, and rice) contributed only 19 percent and livestock, 32 percent.[17] Because most livestock was exported, the dominance of the export sector was pronounced. Warnken characterizes the structure of Nicaraguan agricultural crop production as follows:

> On the one hand, a relatively small proportion of all producers are oriented to the export market, operate relatively large units and produce their product (with the exception of coffee) under relatively high technology levels. On the other hand, a very high proportion of all producers produce for the domestic market on very small units utilizing very low technology levels.[18]

Thus, there was a pronounced dual economy within the agricultural sector.

Although total agricultural production increased at a respectable annual rate of 6.7 percent between 1960–62 and 1969–71 and the average per capita value of agricultural production for the nation was quite high by the 1970s, the structure of the agricultural sector prevented a large part of the rural population from realizing a high level of economic well-being.[19] Rural workers, generally landless, constituted over half of the economically active rural population but accounted for only 7.5 percent of the total gross value of output. The second largest rural group consisted of self-employed and family labor. In aggregate, they received 29 percent of the gross value of production. In contrast, employers accounted for only 3.5 percent of the economically active population yet received 63 percent of the gross income.[20] The dualistic structure of Nicaraguan agriculture that was begun under colonialism and perpetuated under the Somoza dynasty prevented sustained, broad-based economic growth and development and had abominable social consequences. Under the rule of the Somozas, between 50 and 75 percent of the rural population had an insufficient resource base to

17. Philip Warnken, *The Agricultural Development of Nicaragua* (Columbia: University of Missouri Press, 1975), p. 16.

18. Ibid., p. 27.

19. Ibid., pp. 19 and 44.

20. Ibid., p. 44.

create an adequate level of production and consequently lived at minimal subsistence levels.[21]

Beginning in the 1950s, some light industry developed in the wake of the agripastoral sector, the main branches being chemicals and agrochemicals (fertilizer, pesticides, paints, resins). Textile and food processing also developed, as did simple import substitution for such commodities as fertilizer and clothing.[22] The service sector also grew significantly, but it was dominated by "large-scale, nonproductive investments," such as luxury housing, commercial buildings, and other urban real estate.[23] The growth of a nascent industrial sector and of the service sector did not alter the economy's position in the international division of labor. Nicaragua continues to export primarily raw materials (cotton, coffee, beef, sugar) and to import most of the manufactured goods consumed in the country. Agriculture remains the backbone of the economy.

The Insurrection

The inequities and excesses of the Somoza regime led to widespread opposition. With the increasing centralization of not only political power but also economic power in the hands of the dictator and his associates, even the middle-class business sector, which had previously provided the bulk of support for the regime, came to oppose Somoza, especially after the 1972 earthquake that destroyed Managua. During the reconstruction, Somoza's greed in ensuring that his interests benefited most so alienated members of the middle-class business sector that they threw in their lot with any effective opposition to the regime. Somoza's oppression of the traditional middle-class opposition parties resulted unintentionally in the only effective opposition being armed opposition.[24]

Thus, the guerillas of the Sandinista Front for National Liberation (FSLN) benefited most from the emerging atmosphere of militant opposition to the regime. Since the 1960s, they had carried out increas-

21. Ibid.
22. Henri Weber, *Nicaragua: The Sandinista Revolution* (London: Verso Editions, 1981), pp. 23–24.
23. James F. Petras and Morris H. Morley, "Economic Expansion, Political Crisis and U.S. Policy in Central America," *Contemporary Marxism* 3 (Summer 1981), p. 72.
24. Latin American Bureau, *Nicaragua* (London: Latin American Bureau, 1980), pp. 21–23.

ingly successful raids in the countryside and later even in Managua itself. Although the Sandinistas were initially divided into three factions, they ultimately were united under the broader-based faction that favored an immediate military strike against the regime and eventually a political alliance with the rest of the opposition.

The Sandinista attacks, and their call for a broad anti-Somoza front comprising all opposition forces regardless of their political persuasions, galvanized and mobilized the population into fighting an intense and bloody revolution that it ultimately won, despite the brutality of Somoza's national guard. On July 19, 1979, the FSLN assumed power after Somoza left the country. The mobilization of popular opposition against the Somoza regime was especially significant because the radical forces in Nicaragua were among the least advanced in Central America, possessing neither a strong organizational base nor a developed political consciousness within the population.[25]

While the armed opposition of the FSLN brought about the decisive confrontation with Somoza, the struggle to end the dictatorship became an immediate objective of practically all political parties, associations of economic interests, popular organizations, as well as the Sandinista guerilla organization. The diversity of forces that allied to overthrow Somoza was one of the most novel features of the Nicaraguan Revolution. The unwillingness of the Somoza regime to make even the smallest concessions led many moderate groups to align with the FSLN because a peaceful solution to the crisis seemed impossible.

Once it became clear that Somoza's days were numbered, the Carter administration encouraged other political actors to enter into the anti-regime alliance with the hope of neutralizing communist factions within the FSLN. At the same time, the FSLN clearly expressed a need for an alliance with the anti-Somocista "bourgeoisie," not only to get rid of the dictator but also "to begin and support a democratic change after overthrowing Somocismo."[26] The FSLN desire for alliance was probably inevitable because neither it nor any other political organization of the left had the capacity to mobilize the population toward socialist objectives that would permit them to tie the struggle against Somoza to a struggle against the bourgeoisie.[27]

25. R. Burbach and T. Draimin, "Nicaragua's Revolution," *NACLA* (North American Council on Latin America) 24 (May-June 1980), p. 5.

26. Jorge G. Castañeda, *Nicaragua: Contradicciones en la Revolución* (Mexico City: Tiempo Extra Editores, 1980), p. 44.

27. *Inforpress*, 1981, p. N-2.

In committing itself to this alliance, the FSLN had from the beginning the advantage of not deceiving itself: the ally was not a friend, and it had its own interests, distinct and opposed to those of the FSLN; these interests would be to develop a more secure, reformed capitalism. Thus, the alliance contained a fundamental struggle, and the consequences were not a matter of chance: "We are in a card game with the bourgeoisie in which the strongest and most able will win the game."[28] Although members of the bourgeoisie expressed a guarded optimism, they undoubtedly had their own reservations regarding the alliance and aspired to influence the new government to further their own interests.

The New Regime

A month before Somoza's overthrow, the FSLN took the initiative and proposed a provisional government that contained important concessions to other political and economic actors. FSLN leaders announced the formation of a five-member junta, issued a Program of Government outlining policy objectives, and proposed the formation of a thirty-three-member quasi-legislative Council of State that would include members of all political groups that had opposed the dictatorship. The FSLN, because of its initiative, the disarming concessions it offered, the absence of a well-organized alternative source of power, and by virtue of being the military vanguard of the revolution, was able to determine the institutional structure of the new government and define the authority and composition of its organizational units.[29]

The concessions announced in the Program of Government, along with the subsequent appointment of numerous moderates and conservatives to important positions in the new government, led some observers to anticipate a gradual diminution of leftist influence in policymaking. Yet, in fact, the Sandinista leadership, centered in the FSLN's National Directorate (DNC), has not only resisted attempts to compromise the intentions of the FSLN but has also succeeded in tightening leftist control of the government. Equally important, the DNC has established its control over the composition of the new government and dominated the policy-making process while avoiding the use of openly authoritarian tactics, and it has increased its power in a way that has

28. Castañeda, *Nicaragua*, p. 44.
29. Stephen M. Gorman, "Power and Consolidation in the Nicaraguan Revolution," *Journal of Latin American Studies* 13 (May 1981), p. 138.

made it progressively more difficult for other actors to oppose the regime.

The first critical test of the DNC's ability to dominate the national political process was its effort to prevent the five-member Government of National Reconstruction(JGRN) from establishing an independent political existence. The DNC originally appeared to have only two supporters on the junta; however, Sergio Ramírez turned out to be a firm supporter of DNC leadership, giving the DNC a firm majority on the JGRN. The JGRN was never really given any authority by the DNC, and an attempt to establish an independent political existence probably would not have been tolerated. Still, having a majority of supporters on the JGRN enabled the DNC to maintain its control over the composition of the new government and dominate the policy-making process while avoiding a confrontation.[30]

Like the governing junta, the original cabinet appointed by the DNC in late July of 1979 appeared not only to offer important concessions by the Sandinistas, but, in fact, to give five conservatives and moderates a predominance of power. Also, representatives of the private sector were given three of the most sensitive economic ministries: economic planning, industry, and agriculture. Although nominally under the authority of the JGRN, the cabinet actually remained under the full control of the DNC. Conservative officeholders were prevented from consolidating their influence and retarding radical reforms. The ministries were given the opportunity only to implement policy—as opposed to making it. Policy was formulated by the DNC and issued by decree. There was no forum where ministers could present alternative policy proposals, and appointees who opposed DNC policies were replaced with more sympathetic appointees, who were inevitably Sandinistas.[31]

By February 1980, several of the moderates had become radicalized, and most important ministries originally entrusted to conservative businessmen had been put in the hands of two members of the DNC. Commander Henry Ruíz assumed control of the Ministry of Economic Planning, and the ministries of Agriculture and Agrarian Reform were combined under the direction of Commander Jaime Wheelock. These and similar changes produced a very different con-

30. Ibid., pp. 139–142.
31. Ibid.

figuration of the cabinet. In fact, DNC members held all the important ministries after the first year of the revolution.

The moderates and conservatives of the JGRN and the original cabinet were unable to use their positions to undercut the Sandinistas' political support among Nicaraguans or to present policy alternatives largely because of the DNC's calculated delay in creating the quasi-legislative body, the Council of State. Like the JGRN, the Council of State was never intended to be vested with any real authority: it does not have the power to formulate binding legislation and only serves as a forum for discussing issues and for making recommendations. Nevertheless, it could have provided political backing for private sector representatives attempting to curb the power of the DNC, especially since the projected makeup of the council distributed power equally between interests closely identified with the FSLN and those not so identified. Even the slightest political shift to the right by certain constituent groups would have produced a legislative body dominated by moderate and conservative interests.[32]

The Program of Government issued by the DNC in June 1979 called for the formation of a thirty-three-member legislative council representing twenty-three different organizations. The proposed composition was justified as follows: "Such a council will assure an ample representation to the political, economic, and social forces that have contributed to the overthrow of the Somoza dictatorship."[33] However, the DNC decided to postpone formalizing the institution until it could be assured that the council would be under its control. The DNC strengthened its control of a number of older and new mass-based organizations before proposing a new formula for the Council of State. The Council of State was finally established in May 1980. The number of organizations was increased to twenty-nine and the number of representatives, to forty-seven. Organizations either controlled by or closely allied with the FSLN received a definite majority of the forty-seven seats, and Bayardo Arce of the DNC was appointed presiding officer.[34]

The FSLN has sought to provide a support base for its consolidation of power at the highest levels of government by establishing new polit-

32. Ibid.
33. *Encuentro*, 1980, No. 17, p. 33.
34. Department of Social Sciences UNAN, *Curso Sobre la Problemática Actual* (Managua: UNAN, 1980), pp. 85–86.

ical actors throughout society. Parallel organizations have been established to weaken existing organizations (ranging from newspapers to trade unions) that are not necessarily tied to the FSLN. The most difficult and controversial attempt at undermining an established institution has been the formation of a "popular church" to offset the strength of the Catholic church. Equally important, the FSLN has created new institutions where none existed among the urban and rural poor. These new organizations, commonly called "mass organizations," include everything from peasant groups to block committees (CDSs) modeled after Cuba's Committees for the Defense of the Revolution (CDRs).

The FSLN-sponsored organizations have been developed and strengthened through ongoing efforts at political suasion and by channeling government services and goods through them. For example, continued government employment depends on participation in government political organizations. Ration cards are obtained from the neighborhood block committees. Peasants receiving credit from the government-controlled banks are expected to affiliate with government organizations. Although outright coercion to affiliate with these organizations has been rare, there are opportunity costs to not participating. In the absence of coercion, the government's ability to maintain a relative degree of mobilization depends on its continued ability to channel resources to its supporters.

The state-sponsored organizations are strongest in urban areas. First, there is what the Mexican intellectual Octavio Paz has called the organic link between power and cities. Labor unions, the church, economic associations, the media, and the government itself are all centered in urban areas. Second, active support for the revolution has always been strongest in the cities (where the decisive battles were fought). Third, organized opposition to the new regime is likewise most visible and strongest in the urban areas, encouraging the FSLN to concentrate its efforts in principal cities. In contrast, rural organizations are less numerous and less important politically.

At the same time that the FSLN has strengthened its political control, it has also consolidated its hold on the military, capitalizing on the destruction of the national guard by establishing an army loyal to its own interests. With the help of Cuban military advisors, the FSLN has turned an irregular guerilla force into a professional army. The FSLN has strengthened the armed forces by weeding out undesirable soldiers, by training, by procuring improved weapons and supplies, and by developing communication and logistic support capabilities. Special attention has been given to ensuring the loyalty of the troops to the FSLN. Political and cultural sections have been established in all army units and even in the Sandinista police. Political indoctrination was viewed as essential to ensure that the new army "knew whose interests it is protecting and who the enemies of those interests are."[35] In keeping with the goals of the FSLN, the new military has been shielded from potentially nonrevolutionary interests. Offers of training and assistance from the United States, made during the first year of the revolution, were turned down. The destruction of the national guard and the establishment of a new and loyal army drastically reduced the pressures on the new regime and removed the possibility of a coup designed to return the status quo to power, as happened in Chile in 1973.

By the second year of the revolution, the makeup of the new government looked very different from both the Program of Government issued by the FSLN just before the fall of Somoza and the initial post-insurrection government. The FSLN has consolidated its power enough to be in complete control of the government. Moreover, the establishment of a highly politicized army loyal to the FSLN not only defends its accomplishments but also gives it the opportunity to undertake even more ambitious social changes in the future. This expansion of power is especially remarkable because the FSLN has for the most part been able to avoid openly authoritarian tactics. The adroit consolidation of political power in the two years after the revolution is as much of a success for the FSLN as was ending the Somoza dictatorship.

The key to the FSLN's success in consolidating power was its consistent practice of retaining final authority and of delaying, or avoiding altogether, the establishment of institutional structures. The institutional structure that exists in Nicaragua has just emerged from the FSLN's unilateral decisions. Concessions were made to other political actors, but they were all of the type that could be rescinded. The appointment of moderates and conservatives to important government positions is not very consequential when they can be dismissed and replaced at any time. The FSLN has made political changes that are

35. Roberto Sánchez of the Press Office of the Sandinista People's Army, Managua, 2 June 1980, quoted in Gorman, "Power and Consolidation," p. 144.

not particularly significant individually but that, in aggregate, have considerable impact. Furthermore, each change by the FSLN leaves other sectors weaker.[36]

The justification that the FSLN gives for monopolizing political power is that it represents the majority of Nicaraguans, particularly poor workers and peasants. The Sandinistas have constructed huge billboards with such slogans as *El Pueblo Ya Hizo Su Elección: Sandino, Fonseco, FSLN* (The People Have Already Voted: Sandino, Fonseca, FSLN) and *Poder Popular = Poder Sandinista* (Power of the Masses = Sandinista Power).[37] Another example, hardly less modest, comes from one of the commanders of the revolution. Commenting on the large proportion of Sandinistas in the legislative body, the Council of State, Commander Arce said, "This is a Sandinista State; it is a state where the majority of our people subscribe to the political philosophy of Sandinismo, that is why the Council of State has to reflect this majority."[38] The Sandinistas argue that because of the traditional lack of political awareness and the political weakness of the lower classes, they need to maintain their hegemony to ensure that the revolution will be really democratic, benefiting all people and not just a few.

FSLN leaders have consolidated power in Nicaragua for the stated purpose of changing the country. There is no definitive statement of the new regime's specific goals, and, in fact, there may be no specific agenda. At times, pronouncements suggest goals with chiliastic elements. For example, the economic plan for 1980 outlined: "We are setting out on a road to build not only a New Economy, but also a New Man."[39] For the most part, however, wording suggests that goals are largely materialistic—the construction of the new economy. The regime's ambitions have been summarized as (1) restore production disrupted by the insurrection, (2) dismantle the economic base of the old regime, and (3) redistribute income.[40] In brief, the regime seeks to end

36. Superior Council of Private Enterprise (COSEP), *Análisis Sobre la Ejecución del Programa de Gobierno de Reconstrucción Nacional* (Managua: COSEP, 1980), p. 4.

37. *Patria Libre*, no. 13, April 1981, p. 3.

38. Ibid., no. 4, May 1980, p. 22.

39. National Secretary for Propaganda and Political Education, FSLN, *Programa de Reactivación Económica en Beneficio del Pueblo* (Managua: National Secretary for Propaganda and Political Education, FSLN, 1980), p. 31.

40. John A. Booth, *The End and the Beginning: The Nicaraguan Revolution* (Boulder, Colo.: Westview Press, 1982), p. 203.

the inequities that were begun under colonialism and accentuated during the reign of the Somozas.

The consolidation of political power by the FSLN and the concomitant emergence of a strong and unified central government facilitate the formulation and implementation of policies to achieve the desired goal of restructuring Nicaragua. However, the draconian solution of having the state assume complete responsibility for the economy was not feasible, either politically or technically. Consequently, the autonomy of the new regime was from the beginning limited by the state's dependence on economic actors, including many who were opposed to policies that would undermine their economic welfare. As one Sandinista official put it bluntly, "We have to permit the bourgeoisie to reactivate the economy in order to protect the revolution: We must feed the people or they will throw us out like they did Somoza."[41]

The actual outcome of state initiatives thus depends on the dialectical performance of the state and countless economic actors. The manipulation of incipient authority by the FSLN leaves these economic actors without much overt political power, but they have other resources. The internal dynamics of the post-revolutionary era have influenced, and been influenced by, international relations, adding yet another dimension. Given Nicaragua's resources and its historical development, which have led the nation to concentrate on agroexports in the international division of labor, the dynamics of the post-revolutionary era have been most pronounced in rural Nicaragua.

The Revolution and Rural Nicaragua

Because agriculture is so important to the economy, the new regime sees agrarian reform as the foundation of the revolution. An extra sense of urgency for agricultural development has come from the need to restore domestic food supplies and rebuild the export sector, both of which were disrupted by the revolution. The importance of the rural sector was underlined by the establishment, barely a week after the Sandinistas marched into Managua, of the Nicaraguan Institute for Agrarian Reform (INRA), to be headed by a member of the National Directorate of the FSLN.

Although there has been considerable state activity in the agricul-

41. Ibid., p. 197.

Table 1   *Production of Agricultural Products by Form of Ownership, 1979–80*

	State Sector (%)	Small Producers (%)	Large Producers (%)
Cotton	20.0	18.0	62.0
Coffee	15.0	30.0	55.0
Livestock	15.0	73.0	12.0
Maize	8.7	87.2	4.1
Beans	17.0	79.1	3.8

SOURCE: Center for the Study of Agrarian Reform (CIERA), "Significación de la reforma agraria" (Managua, 1980, Mimeographed).

NOTE: Although the table is from a government source, the figures can be taken as only approximate. In particular, small producers' stated contributions to cotton production are too high.

tural sector, peasant proprietors (or small farmers) and largely private commercial farms have retained an important role in the economy. The different sectors' shares in the production of principal crops can be seen in Table 1. The role of the state in the agricultural sector and its relationship to small and large producers can be summarized as follows:

1. expropriation of land belonging to Somoza and his associates and management of the land by the state as collective farms;

2. organization of small farmers into various types of cooperatives to facilitate state control and provision of credit and other inputs;

3. regulation and cajoling of large private farmers in order to meet state goals of improving the welfare of rural workers and increasing production.

Within weeks of its victory, the new government drastically altered the land tenure structure in Nicaragua through the wholesale confiscation of the landed estates owned by Somoza and his associates. It was decided that once acquired by the state, these lands could be held and worked only through collective forms of farming, such as production cooperatives or state farms; they would not be redistributed as individual private parcels.[42] As a result of the confiscations, INRA, later merged with the Ministry of Agriculture to form the Ministry of Agriculture and Agrarian Reform (MIDINRA), controlled about 25 percent of Nicaragua's arable land, most of it fertile and productive. This land was reorganized in two forms: (1) large integrated enterprises, such as coffee plantations with mills attached, which were placed under the control of Agro-INRA, and (2) farms and scattered plots with few if any processing facilities, which were grouped into agricultural complexes, which in turn were broken down into production units run by MIDINRA administrators. There were 170 of these complexes, composed of twenty-two hundred production units covering two million acres. Agro-INRA, by comparison, was responsible only for ninety thousand acres.[43]

Peasant proprietors were organized under the National Committee for Small Producers. Another branch of MIDINRA, Pro-Campo, gave credit and technical and marketing assistance and encouraged peasants to set up cooperatives. Some cooperatives simply distributed credit, bought inputs, or marketed crops; others were production units. The government maintained that cooperatives allowed more comprehensive planning of the agricultural sector and were the best solution to the continuing problem of subdivision of land into smaller and uneconomical plots. Cooperatives, however, would be voluntary and would proceed by stages, beginning with credit, marketing, and services and only later involving production.[44]

Despite the government's confiscation and subsequent management of the large estates of Somoza and his associates, large producers were to continue playing an important role in the agricultural sector. Large private commercial farms concentrating on such export crops as cotton, coffee, cattle, and sugar accounted for 64.5 percent of Nicaragua's cultivable land.[45] As can be expected, a tense and sometimes contradictory relationship has existed between this private sector and the new revolutionary government. Although the government has expressed a desire for a mixed economy with an active private sector, it

42. David Kaimowitz and Joseph Thome, *Nicaragua's Agrarian Reform: The First Year (1979–1980)* (Madison: Land Tenure Center, University of Wisconsin-Madison, 1981), p. 7.
43. *Latin American Weekly Report*, 22 August 1980, p. 9.
44. Kaimowitz and Thome, *Nicaragua's Agrarian Reform*, p. 19.
45. Ibid., p. 21.

has used a combination of economic incentives, controls, and threats to prompt the private sector to meet the revolution's goals as interpreted by the FSLN.[46]

Other agricultural policies undertaken that affected both small and large producers were the nationalization of all marketing channels for agricultural exports, direct government purchase and sale of basic grains, and control of rents. State-operated foreign trade companies were established for exporting coffee, cotton, sugar, meat, and fish, as well as for importing pesticides, fertilizers, and other agricultural inputs. State control over foreign trade gave the government direct control over this crucial sector of the economy and made it possible to tax that sector directly. The government also achieved control over consumer prices for basic foodstuffs, though much of the internal marketing of basic foods remained in private hands.[47]

The relative ease with which the agrarian reform began is probably largely explained in the following passage from a Land Tenure Center report:

> Few, if any, governments have been able to start an agrarian reform with an almost costless and instant nationalization of vast and productive landholdings. Even more unique, this was achieved without alienating the bulk of the landowning class, most of whom despised the Somoza clan. Moreover, the very fact that the government had to swallow such a large morsel all at once gave the large landowners a certain measure of security, at least for a while.[48]

The success of agrarian reform depends to a large extent on the government's ability to maintain a delicate balance between the interests of the state sector, consumers, rural workers and peasants, and the large commercial farmers and ranchers. Four representative sectors of rural Nicaragua will be examined in detail to determine how these conflicts of interest have been resolved in the critical early years of the post-revolutionary era.

46. Ibid., p. 22.
47. Solon Barraclough, "Report of the IFAD Special Programming Mission to Nicaragua" (Managua, 1980, Mimeographed).
48. Kaimowitz and Thome, *Nicaragua's Agrarian Reform*, p. 8.

3

The Rural Elite
Privilege, Production, and Revolution

POST-REVOLUTIONARY regimes depend on economic performance. It is almost axiomatic, though, that important centers of production will be in the hands of those who are the target of the revolution, or who are at least antagonistic to it, and that at least initially the state will be unable to assume complete responsibility for the production of essential goods and services. Understanding this dilemma and how it is resolved provides insights into post-revolutionary regimes in the developing world. Economic elites are often unwilling to maintain production during attempts at radical structural change because of a loss of short-term incentives as a result of either direct or indirect government policies. Also, there is likely to be uncertainty about future state policies. The withholding of expected investments and the partial or total withdrawal from production inevitably provokes the government, setting off a chain of aggressive state policies and defensive counterstrategies on the part of the private sector. [1]

Tension and uncertainty between the state and the private sector are further compounded by the difficult task of evaluating private sector compliance with state expectations and state-set norms. Private producers, confronting a cohesive and militant state, most often respond to ill-regarded policies not with open confrontation tactics but with passive noncompliance, evasion, deception, flight, and even subtle sabotage. These tacit forms of class struggle require little or no coor-

1. Arturo Valenzuela, *Chile* (Baltimore: Johns Hopkins University Press, 1978), pp. 70 and 77.

45

dination or planning. An attempt is typically made to avoid any direct symbolic confrontation with authority because the perpetrators' safety lies in their anonymity.[2] The state is likely to be confronted with such difficult questions as, "Does a farmer have low yields because of excessive cost cutting or because it was a 'bad year'?"

This chapter explores the circumstances under which members of a privileged social class or group will continue to produce in the aftermath of a revolution by examining the experience of Nicaraguan cotton producers. Before the revolution of 1979, cotton was the country's largest foreign-exchange earner and an important source of employment. But production was highly concentrated, and the Sandinistas had long criticized this concentration. This chapter attempts to identify, for the post-revolutionary period, factors that have both discouraged and encouraged cotton production, by analyzing producers' reactions to various government policies and the survival strategies they have developed in response to those policies.

Cotton Production in Nicaragua

Although coffee was the earliest basis of capital accumulation in Nicaragua, beginning in the late 1950s its importance to the economy was surpassed by cotton. In the 1960s, cotton became the largest source of rural employment and the largest foreign-exchange earner, providing an estimated 37 percent of rural employment and 35 percent of Nicaragua's foreign-exchange earnings. Cotton was by far the most modern sector of the rural economy. During the early 1970s, cotton absorbed an estimated 85 percent of imported agricultural inputs. The modernization of cultivation contributed to a 268 percent increase in production between 1960 and 1978 and propelled Nicaragua into the position of the world's tenth largest cotton producer, with yields above the world average. Cotton was the foundation of the Nicaraguan economy.[3]

Although cotton was the strength and pride of the previous regime, it was strongly criticized by the Sandinistas. Orlando Nuñez, now di-

2. This conceptualization is from James C. Scott, *Everyday Forms of Peasant Resistance* (New Haven, Conn.: Yale University Press, forthcoming).

3. For a discussion of the development of cotton production in Nicaragua, see National Bank of Nicaragua, *Estudio de la Economía del Algodón en Nicaragua* (Managua: National Bank of Nicaragua, 1965); Central Bank of Nicaragua, *Análisis Sobre las Perspectivas Algodoneras en Nicaragua* (Managua: Central Bank of Nicaragua, 1978).

rector of the Center for the Study of Agrarian Reform (CIERA), outlined the criticisms of the Sandinistas in his book *El Somocismo y el Modelo Capitalista Agroexportador:*

> The Nicaraguan capitalist economy is fundamentally based on the activities of agro-exportation, and the dominant role within this sector is played by capitalist production. From 1950 to date, the cultivation of cotton has displaced traditional products with respect to area planted, monopolization of credit, infrastructure, modern technology, influence in the incipient industrialization of the country, use of salaried labor, monopolization of capital, generation of foreign exchange for the country, etc., etc.[4]

> Cotton production makes the Nicaraguan economy definitively a capitalist economy whose model of accumulation shares the following characteristics: Concentration of the means of production (land) and seasonal proletarianization with a limited internal market and with an incipient industrialization; phenomena that block access to land and employment to the majority of the labor force.[5]

As is clear from the quotes, the criticisms of cotton cultivation were that it (1) displaced traditional agriculture, (2) monopolized government services, and (3) greatly accentuated the inequitable distribution of employment and income. Cotton cultivation was also criticized for a fourth reason—it deepened involvement in the world market.[6]

Studying the fate of cotton under the revolution is illuminating, given the prerevolutionary importance of cotton to the economy and the Sandinistas' attitudes toward this sector. Analyzing the reaction of the most advanced producers of the agricultural sector to the revolution is as worthwhile as evaluating the policies of the new regime toward cotton producers.

Characteristics of Cotton Producers

Cotton producers vary in the amount of land they cultivate. Table 2 outlines the landholdings of cotton producers for 1977–78. There are small, medium, and large producers. However, despite the

---

4. Orlando Núñez, *El Somocismo y el Modelo Capitalista Agroexportador* (Managua: Dept. de Ciencas Sociales de la Universidad Nacional Autónoma de Nicaragua, 1981), p. 17.
5. Ibid., p. 6.
6. Ibid.

Table 2   *Number of Cotton Producers by Area Harvested, 1977–78*

Cotton Producers' Landholdings (in manzanas)	Number of Producers	Manzanas Harvested
1–4	1,379	4,458
5–9	1,443	9,057
10–19	1,113	13,573
20–29	537	11,498
30–39	267	8,146
40–49	194	7,554
50–99	617	36,665
100–199	451	52,781
200–299	207	43,456
300–399	94	28,320
400–499	43	16,780
500–999	78	44,326
1,000 and Above	19	26,786
Total	6,442	303,400

SOURCE: National Cotton Commission, as reported in Central Bank of Nicaragua, *Informe Anual 1978* (Managua: Central Bank of Nicaragua, 1980), p. 91.

existence of numerous small producers, cotton cultivation has always been highly concentrated. In 1977–78, 83 percent of land planted in cotton was in farms of fifty manzanas or more.[7] Thus, cotton is much more highly concentrated than Nicaragua's historic export crop, coffee. There are an estimated twenty-seven thousand coffee producers in Nicaragua, and 85 percent of them are small producers.

Cotton producers also differ from coffee producers in that there are not noticeable variances in technology among small, medium, and large producers. Cotton is cultivated using only a rather high level of technology. Consequently, cost structures and yields do not differ appreciably.[8] More extensive and efficient cultivation practices allow many large cotton producers to attain yields of forty quintals per man-

7. One manzana (mz) = 0.705 hectares.
8. Central American Institute of Business Administration (INCAE), "Nicaragua: Estudio de la Situación del Empleo, la Absorción de la Mano de Obra y Otros Aspectos en Fincas y Productores de Café y Algodón" (Managua, July 1982, Mimeographed), p. 151.

zana instead of the thirty quintals many small producers receive.[9] This difference is not inconsequential, but it is nothing like the differences in coffee yields, where large modernized producers have yields five or six times those of small traditional producers.

The modernization of cotton production in Nicaragua not only generated wealth and employment but also spawned a new agricultural elite, which possessed valuable technical and managerial skills and differed from the stereotype of the nineteenth-century Latin American landlord because it "produced" as well as "consumed." According to an INCAE survey, large cotton producers tend to be well educated and trained, with an average of twenty years of experience cultivating cotton.[10] An anecdote testifies to the acknowledged skills of cotton producers: when the state recently confiscated a cotton farm in the department of Masaya, authorities took the unusual step of asking a neighboring cotton producer to manage the farm.

The "cotton boom" was facilitated and reinforced by government support, principally through the construction of infrastructure and the provision of credit. The lowlands of the Pacific coast, where cotton is cultivated, present few barriers to transportation, and an excellent road system was established in the 1950s and 1960s. The profit margins in cotton likewise attracted credit. The INCAE survey reaveals that before the revolution, 94 percent of producers received credit.[11] This figure may be somewhat inflated, but cotton clearly received a much higher percentage of financing than other crops in Nicaragua.

Policies of the New Regime Toward the Cotton Sector

The FSLN's 1979 triumph profoundly scared cotton producers. Although the Somoza family did not cultivate cotton, cotton producers were widely seen as a conspicuous part of the dominant class, or the bourgeoisie. They watched with trepidation as nearly 17 percent of the area devoted to cotton cultivation was confiscated and deemed "property of the people." Most of the producers thus affected were acknowledged to have links with the previous regime, but some confiscations were carried out to appease militant laborers or because the

9. One quintal (qq) = 46 kilos or 100 pounds.
10. INCAE, "Nicaragua," p. 156.
11. Ibid., p. 206.

land was near urban centers where there was a clamor for land. Producers viewed the establishment of a government monopsony for cotton with suspicion. Finally, there was concern over FSLN leaders' fiery rhetoric and the government's ultimate composition and intentions.

The new regime sought through the expropriations to seize the assets of those associated with the excesses of the previous regime. The Somoza regime had so little legitimacy that the act appeared to most Nicaraguans to be equivalent to reclaiming stolen property. The seizure of cotton estates for other reasons—inevitably tied to pressure from peasants and laborers—was not publicly discussed and probably not even planned. The establishment of a government monopsony for cotton was carried out to give the government complete control over the valuable foreign exchange generated by cotton exports and to broaden the state's taxation power.[12] The new regime's immediate policies were undertaken to ensure that the sector would be purged of its "criminal" elements and that the wealth generated by the sector would be made available to meet the needs of "all Nicaraguans" as interpreted by the FSLN.

The disruptions engendered by the fighting, the arbitrary land seizures that accompanied the expropriation of the Somocistas' farms, and the general fears of the revolutionary process all contributed to a notable decrease in production. The area cultivated in cotton fell from 303,400 manzanas in 1977–78 to 135,900 in 1980–81, a 55 percent decrease.[13] Because cotton had been the largest generator of the foreign exchange so important to a small state like Nicaragua, the drop in production presented a grave threat to the country. Furthermore, cotton production showed little sign of recovering to its prerevolution status.

The necessity of avoiding a continued reduction in cotton production complicated the FSLN's policies toward private cotton producers. A set of specific policies that suggest a change in attitude on the part of the FSLN cannot be pinpointed. Instead, the revolutionary leaders' attitudes became increasingly ambiguous. Their opinion of cotton pro-

12. For an analysis of the state marketing monopsony, see Carlos Guillermo Sequeira, "State and Private Marketing Arrangements in the Agricultural Export Industries: The Case of Nicaragua's Coffee and Cotton" (Ph.D. dissertation, Harvard University, 1981).

13. Union of Nicaraguan Agricultural Producers (UPANIC), "Estudios Económicos" (Managua, 1983, Mimeographed). The fall in cotton production in 1978–79 was accompanied by a decline in the number of every size of producer—small, medium, and large.

ducers never changed, but as the FSLN got involved in administration, its leaders realized that pragmatic considerations could not be overlooked. The most pressing concern has been a continuing crisis in the balance of payments; the value of imports has consistently been roughly double the value of exports since the revolution.[14]

Because the state has been unable—and perhaps unwilling—to assume complete responsibility for cotton production, it has little choice but to attempt to meet the conditions necessary to keep the private sector producing and, ideally, to persuade it to increase production. The new regime has had to be conciliatory to cotton producers not only because of the importance of the crop in generating foreign exchange, but also because of both the nature of cotton production and the "mobility" of cotton producers. Unlike coffee, cotton is planted annually, and the decision to invest or not to invest in cotton production can be made yearly. Also, as might be expected given their class status, most cotton growers are economically and socially mobile. An estimated 40 percent of cotton has historically been cultivated on rented land, and, as mentioned earlier, nearly all cotton production was previously financed by credit.[15] Moreover, cotton growers tend to have the education and resources necessary to switch occupations—or even to emigrate.

Cotton producers' mobility is acknowledged in an internal government document:

> Because the crop is for the most part in the hands of large cotton producers, the fundamental criterion that determines the working of the subsystem is the financial return of the crop for the large producers. This is to say that the principal variables are short-term economic variables: the anticipated price of cotton, cost of inputs and labor, taxation, and credit conditions. The latter factor plays a very important role given that cotton production is based on circulatory capital, with very little fixed capital. The producer does not use his own capital, but instead money borrowed on a short-term basis.[16]

14. Marc Lindenberg, "Political Perspectives in Central America 1983/84" (Managua, 1983, Mimeographed).

15. Much of the land rented was actually held by cotton producers' relatives. This practice was adopted so that additional credit could be obtained for alleged rental costs.

16. Ministry of Agriculture and Agrarian Reform (MIDINRA), "Las Políticas para el Sector Agropecuario; Presentación por Subsistemas Productivos" (Managua, 1982, Mimeographed), p. 28.

Other agricultural producers—especially marginal peasants cultivating basic grains—do not have the same mobility.

The new regime has a wide range of policy instruments at its command to provide the conditions necessary for cotton producers to continue growing cotton and, at the same time, to ensure that cotton producers do not realize more of a gain than the government deems appropriate. An internal government document lists these four policy instruments: availability of land, credit, prices, and salaries and working conditions.[17] The most extensive policy instrument, and the one easiest to manipulate, is the control of prices. As the document asserts, "The state can regulate almost all of the prices within the subsystem."[18] Prices for nearly all inputs, as well as the price paid for the cotton produced, can be regulated. The report concludes that availability of credit is most important for maintaining cotton production.[19]

Because the government has assumed complete control of foreign trade, it is now responsible for providing the extensive imported inputs needed for cotton production. Although control of imported agricultural inputs can be seen as yet another policy instrument, it has proven to be little more than a burden. Problems of administration, as well as the shortage of foreign exchange, have often impeded the timely provision of needed agricultural inputs.[20] For example, in the harvest of 1981–82, many of the trailers that transport cotton could not be used because of an acute shortage of tires. The government's shifting of trade from capitalist countries to the Soviet Union and its allies has also caused problems.[21]

In addition to providing needed agricultural inputs, the government devotes considerable resources to computing the amount of credit necessary for cotton production and the price it will pay cotton producers for their harvests. This is a difficult task because of the tension between the desire to limit the earnings of a class to whom the revolution—as interpreted by the FSLN—owes nothing and the realization that producers will not cultivate cotton in the absence of financial incentives. Three factors further complicate the government's task:

17. Ibid., pp. 31–35.
18. Ibid., p. 32.
19. Ibid., p. 30.
20. INCAE, "Nicaragua," p. 233.
21. Lindenberg, "Political Perspectives."

Table 3   *Cost of and Returns from Cotton, 1981–82*

Yield (qq/mz)	Total Cost (C$/mz)	Foreign Exchange Generated (U.S.$/mz)	Net Profit (C$/mz)
28	8,997	383	−1,443
29	9,060	408	−1,201
30	9,122	432	−959
31	9,185	457	−717
32	9,247	481	−475
33	9,310	506	−233
34	9,372	531	9
35	9,435	555	251
36	9,497	580	493
37	9,560	604	735
38	9,622	629	977

SOURCE: Ministry of Agriculture and Agrarian Reform (MIDINRA), "Costos de Oportunidad de la Producción de Algodón" (Managua, 1982, Mimeographed).

NOTE: Both cost and returns are based on a price of C$1,000/qq. All estates included are larger than seventy-five manzanas.

1. Cotton production is inherently risky; yields (and earnings) have always varied, depending principally on insects and climate.

2. In the post-revolutionary period, international prices for cotton have been low.

3. There has been a predictable attempt on the part of private producers to report inflated costs so as to secure increased credit and higher government prices for their harvests.

Perhaps precisely because of these difficulties, the government takes care to follow production costs closely.

Table 3 details government calculations on the cost of and returns from cotton for the 1981–82 agricultural season. Producers' incomes are calculated for a series of different yields under the assumption of a price to producers of C$1,000 per quintal. Profitability clearly depends primarily on yield. Table 4 highlights the production of cotton since the revolution. The reported average yield for 1980–81 was

Table 4   *Cotton Production by Agricultural Season, 1978–83*

	1978–79	1979–80	1980–81	1981–82	1982–83
Area (thousands of mz)	248.2	54.6	134.6	132.8	129.0
Yield (qq)	32.8	24.6	36.2	30.8	35.9
Production (thousands of qq)	8,152.4	1,344.7	4,878.6	4,081.0	4,628.0
Price paid (C$/qq)	327.5	467.6	720.0	964.0	1,000.0

SOURCE: Union of Nicaraguan Agricultural Products (UPANIC), "Estudios Económicos" (Managua: UPANIC, 1983, Mimeographed).

30.8 quintals per manzana. Under the assumptions of Table 3, producers lost money while the government earned considerable foreign exchange.

The most interesting facet of Table 3 is the price paid to producers. The Nicaraguan government reportedly sold the country's cotton harvest on the international market (principally to Japan, China, and Taiwan) for U.S.$63 a quintal. Given the prevailing official exchange rate, that would suggest a price to domestic producers of C$630. Nicaraguan cotton producers were not paid the C$1,000 that Table 3 implies, but they were paid close to it—C$964. In February 1982, the government announced an incentive program to boost agricultural exports.[22] Sugar, beef, and cotton were affected, with cotton receiving the largest percentage price increase. Under a rather complicated formula, the price paid to cotton producers was effectively raised to C$964, the equivalent of valuing cotton at an exchange rate of C$15 to U.S.$1.

Since the government has greatly overvalued the cordoba, the price increase is not as significant as it might initially appear. On the legal, parallel exchange market, the cordoba has about a third of the value ascribed by the official exchange rate, and on the "black" market, it is worth only an eighth of its official value.[23] The sharp decline in the

22. *Barricada*, 9 February 1982; *El Nuevo Diario*, 9 February 1982.
23. As of the fourth anniversary of the revolution, July 1983.

value of the cordoba, inflation, and scarcities have markedly diminished the value of any nominal income that producers earn. As one producer bluntly put it, "Here you only earn paper." Still, other agricultural producers—including peasants—have had selling prices for their crops based on a ten to one exchange rate. The explanation for why cotton producers have received preferential treatment is to be found in the third column of Table 3—the foreign exchange cotton generates—and in the aforementioned mobility of cotton producers.

In the 1982–83 agricultural season, the area planted in cotton fell slightly, from 132.8 thousand manzanas to 129 thousand manzanas. Yields, however, were quite high—an average of thirty-six quintals per manzana. The high yield is attributed to extremely favorable weather, and not to improved technology or efficiency.[24] The selling price was virtually unchanged, but because production costs rose only modestly from 1980–81 (in part because the government limited wage increases), many producers realized a gain for the year. Nonetheless, cotton growers remain pessimistic because the value of their nominal income is considered low and because confiscations that they feel are unjustifiable continue.[25]

Cotton producers have not only been tempted with a "carrot" of financial incentives; they have also been threatened with a "stick" of confiscation if they do not produce. On July 19, 1981, the second anniversary of the triumph of the FSLN, the new regime announced a stringent new "decapitalization" law. Decapitalization refers to disinvestment through such means as allowing plant and machinery to run down while profits are pocketed or taking out low-interest government loans designed to stimulate profits and converting the funds to dollars to be sent abroad.[26] Concomitantly, the agrarian reform was clarified and strengthened.[27] Its central thrust was that unused land would be subject to expropriation. For cotton growers, the message of the two laws was "utilize your farms fully and efficiently or lose them."

Finally, government policy toward the cotton sector has involved the government itself growing cotton on expropriated land. According

24. MIDINRA, *Boletín Agrometeorológico Número 130* (Managua, May 1983).

25. INCAE, "Nicaragua," p. 233.

26. Dennis Gilbert, "The Bourgeoisie in the Nicaraguan Revolution," unpublished paper presented at the South Eastern Conference on Latin American Studies, San Juan, Puerto Rico, April 1983, pp. 14–15.

27. MIDINRA, *Marco Jurídico de la Reforma Agraria Nicaragüense* (Managua: MIDINRA, 1982).

to an internal government document, the state now holds 17 percent of the land in cotton cultivation, although other figures suggest that it may be as high as 22 percent.[28] Information on the performance of the state farms is sketchy and often unreliable. The little information available suggests that state farms have faced the same problems as private farms, ranging from shortages of spare parts for machinery to labor indiscipline. The consensus is that state farms have had roughly the same yields as the private sector, but at a much higher cost.[29] Because confiscations have continued, the state sector will be of increasing importance. However, for the present—and for the foreseeable future— the state's attention focuses on the large producers who cultivate 77 percent of Nicaragua's cotton acreage (small producers cultivate 6 percent).[30]

The Reaction of Private Cotton Growers

Some cotton growers joined the effort to oust Somoza, and probably nearly all were glad to see the collapse of the dictatorship. However, with the consolidation of the Sandinistas' power, cotton growers and other members of the "bourgeoisie" began to fear for their futures.[31] They increasingly felt that they were only accommodated because of their contribution to the economy, and once they could be dispensed with, they would be finished. Asked what the government wanted from the private sector, an entrepreneur replied, "Obey. Produce as long as I want you to. I'll cut your throat when I want. Be my servant. Do as I say until I'm ready to dispose of you."[32] Such an attitude is common among Nicaragua's large agricultural producers.[33]

As the prospects for large private cotton growers have dimmed, so

28. MIDINRA, "Las Políticas para el Sector Agropecuario," p. 26.
29. A similar trend is reported during Allende's regime. See David Morawetz, "Economic Lessons from Some Small Socialist Developing Countries," *World Development* 8 (May-June 1980), p. 356.
30. MIDINRA, "Las Políticas para el Sector Agropecuario," p. 26.
31. See Stephen M. Gorman, "Power and Consolidation in the Nicaraguan Revolution," *Journal of Latin American Studies* 13 (May 1981), pp. 133–149.
32. Gilbert, "The Bourgeoisie in the Nicaraguan Revolution," pp. 14–15.
33. A survey conducted in 1983 found that 100 percent of cotton producers interviewed feared expropriation. Alvaro F. Velázquez P., "Estudio Comparativo Sobre la Problemática de la Producción Algodonera Entre los Ciclos Agrícolas 77/78 y 82/83" (Lic. thesis, Instituto Tecnológico y de Estudios Superiores de Monterrey, 1983).

have their options. Whereas cotton land once commanded high prices (even by U.S. standards) and the cordoba could be freely exchanged for U.S. dollars at a favorable rate, there is now no market for cotton farms, and the cordoba is worth only a small fraction of its previous value. One well-known family with substantial investments has made it known that they are not leaving Nicaragua until the Sandinistas take away their name; however, most cotton growers probably would leave if they could "cash out" as they could before the revolution. Because that is no longer an option, there is little to do other than get along as best they can, holding onto their land and hoping for a better future.

Although cotton producers do not snub the financial incentives offered by the government, they do not find them compelling. As the government's own figures attest (in Table 3), making a profit cultivating cotton in post-revolutionary Nicaragua has been difficult. Furthermore, producers maintain that costs often rise unexpectedly above government projections because of government shortcomings. For example, if government agencies do not have a part needed to repair machinery, a producer must often go to great lengths and expense to secure the part himself.[34] Producers often buy dollars on the black market and then travel to neighboring Costa Rica to buy needed spare parts. Or, if insecticides are ineffective, many more applications are necessary than is ordinarily the case. Also, labor costs are often higher because of labor indiscipline and shortages precipitated by the revolution.

A few cotton producers are said to have made some money cultivating cotton, but most have not. Problems such as those previously described are blamed, as are low prices. While international prices are low, the government's monopsony of cotton, and its policy of overvaluing the cordoba result in producers receiving an even lower price than they might expect. Although cotton production has fallen recently throughout Central America, Nicaraguan cotton producers do not feel this is primarily a result of international prices.[35] Many are doubtful they would see any benefits even from higher prices, given the government's present policies.

34. Ibid.
35. INCAE, "Nicaragua," p. 233. The relationship between international cotton prices and the development of the Nicaraguan cotton sector is discussed in Pedro Belli, "An Inquiry Concerning the Growth of Cotton Farming in Nicaragua" (Ph.D. dissertation, University of California, Berkeley, 1968).

Some producers presently manage to realize some gain by surreptitiously reducing their expenses and pocketing part of the credit they receive from the government.[36] For example, they may apply only half of the suggested fertilizer applications. Other tasks will be reduced wherever possible. Yields undoubtedly fall, but the producer can claim that factors beyond his control are responsible and ask for an extension in paying his debt. The practice has been facilitated by the government's leniency toward unpaid credit obligations.

There is some awareness in government circles of the cotton producers' tactics. As an internal government document states: "There are strong grounds to support the presumption that the costs used to compute credit under the present methodology include disguised elements of gain, which producers 'live' on."[37] Although the practice is said to be widespread, and undoubtedly has contributed to a reduction in yields, the government cannot easily combat it. The state has little basis or ability to monitor operating costs in the private sector. In fact, producers claim the high operating costs of state farms aid them in their negotiations with the state over credit. Also, cotton producers often do face higher than anticipated costs, as previously outlined, and diverse problems that result in lower yields.

An alternative strategy pursued by some cotton growers is to switch to cultivating sorghum. There is no way of knowing just how many have adopted this strategy, but statistics on sorghum production suggest that the number is considerable.[38] Cotton producers adopting this strategy do not earn higher returns, but they have fewer headaches because sorghum is easy to cultivate, and they can claim to be using their land. By telling many cotton producers that they can receive credit only for cultivating cotton, the government is trying to discourage them from cultivating sorghum because the crop generates very little foreign exchange.

Producers cannot make much money by cultivating cotton efficiently and in good faith, or even by cutting costs and pocketing part of the credit they receive. Still, if they are already comfortably situated, they can get by—at least until they need to begin replacing such items as machinery and vehicles. The reason most of them continue to

36. It is impossible to measure how widespread this practice is.
37. MIDINRA, "Diagnóstico de la Situación del Sector" (Managua, 1982, Mimeographed), p. 12.
38. UPANIC, "Estudios Económicos."

cultivate cotton, and even to stay in Nicaragua, is the "stick" the government holds over them—the threat of confiscation. Producers know that if they do not cultivate their farms, the farms will be expropriated. Many feel that if they lose their land, they will never again be as well off, so they stay and hope for better times—or, more specifically, for a change of regimes.

Cotton producers, and by extension cotton production, are clearly in a precarious position. The government understands the need for the contribution they make to the national economy, but supporting cotton producers goes against its ideology. Government policy is hence inescapably contradictory toward this sector. Symbolically, the official logotype of the fourth anniversary of the Nicaraguan Revolution shows an arabic numeral four adorned with an automatic rifle and cotton pods.

Cotton producers, for their part, disdain the Sandinistas and are sure that the commanding National Directorate of the FSLN wants to do away with the private sector. The only question in their minds is when. For the moment, cotton producers are torn between the realization that "there is money to be made in every tragedy" and Lenin's sobering adage that "capitalists will make the very rope they will be hanged by."

Given the tension between cotton producers and the state, cotton production is not going to regain its dynamism or even reattain prerevolutionary levels. Even an increase in world prices is unlikely to have much of a salutary effect on present production levels. However, given the state's desperate need for foreign exchange and its consequent willingness to finance cotton production, private cotton growers are unlikely to walk away from their coveted farms. Thus, at least until the fragile balance between the new regime and cotton producers is upset, cotton production is likely to remain more or less where it is now— severely depressed but still a major contributor to the Nicaraguan economy.

Conclusions

The level of cotton production in post-revolutionary Nicaragua, which has resulted from calculated individual decisions on the part of cotton producers, shows both the limits and the possibilities of a privileged social class or group maintaining production in the aftermath of a revolution. The importance of predictability to the "private sector" is underscored. Paramount to this climate of predictability is a clear definition of the respective roles of the private and public sectors. Nothing is as dangerous to the confidence of individual producers as the conviction that the state's actions are arbitrary, especially if—as in the case of Nicaragua—there is no effective judicial recourse. This situation is all the worse if the attitude of the revolutionary regime is inherently hostile to the social group in question. Many, if not most, Nicaraguan cotton producers are favorably disposed to the central tenet of the country's agrarian reform, which is based not on an acreage ceiling but on whether or not the land is being productively used. The events that have unnerved cotton producers are confiscations that are interpreted as being unwarranted according to the law.

In the absence of at least a modicum of confidence in the future, there will be no individual investment. However, a combination of monetary incentives and a nearly complete absence of risk in the short run can be expected to maintain production, particularly if the absence of production results in confiscation. Of singular importance in the short term is credit availability, which eliminates risk. Nicaraguan cotton producers will not invest their money for a single agricultural season, but if credit covers their expenses—including an allocation for managerial input—existing production will largely be maintained. Credit, however, can be subject to the same fraud as tax payments, posing an added administrative burden for the state.

The ratio between costs and revenues remains important, but it becomes secondary. Nicaragua's experience suggests that price incentives can be nullified if the national economy is beset by serious problems that markedly reduce the value of the national currency. It reinforces the finding that this can likewise happen from a heavy "tax" disguised as a greatly overvalued exchange rate.[39] Still, Nicaraguan cotton producers have been the most successful of agricultural producers in obtaining government price concessions. This success implies that prices for producers' outputs depend not on their class status—as revolutionary rhetoric might suggest—but on (1) the importance of the crop to the national economy, and (2) the elasticity of supply.

A revolutionary regime is aided in its efforts to maintain production

39. Robert H. Bates, *Markets and States in Tropical Africa: The Political Basis of Agricultural Policies* (Berkeley and Los Angeles: University of California Press, 1981).

by the fact that, as the prospects for producers decline, so does the value of their fixed capital. In other words, as the incentive to abandon production increases, so does the cost from capital loss. In Nicaragua, cotton estates can be sold for only a tenth of their prerevolutionary value (in real terms)—if they can be sold at all. This restriction provides a strong stimulus for not leaving cotton production, especially because most cotton producers are advanced in age. The inability to emigrate with capital has likewise slowed the flight of white settlers from Zimbabwe.[40]

In addition to the ability to offer credit and monitor prices, the state also has the power to confiscate. This "policy instrument"—in reality, an instrument of coercion—can not only transfer unproductive assets to productive use by the state, but can also intimidate producers into utilizing their capital instead of sitting on their hands. But this policy instrument should be used cautiously and within well-defined limits so as to avoid evoking widespread panic and pessimism among producers who otherwise might be disposed to maintain production. If handled clumsily, the threat of confiscation can do more harm than good.[41] The same can be said, in general, for all government policies in a post-revolutionary epoch aimed at productive sectors, but especially for those controlled by social classes or groups antagonistic to the revolution.

    40. Jeffrey Davidow, *Dealing with International Crisis: Lessons from Zimbabwe*, Occasional Paper 34 (Musatine, Iowa: Stanley Foundation, 1983), p. 13.
    41. Mozambique's experience suggests the damage that can result from abrupt elite flight as a result of fear and uncertainty. Allen Isaacman and Barbara Isaacman, *Mozambique: From Colonialism to Revolution, 1900–1982* (Boulder, Colo.: Westview Press, 1983), chap. 7.

4

Small Agroexporters
Production Without Mobility

THE STRATUM of rural Nicaragua that can perhaps provide the most insight into the dynamics of the Nicaraguan Revolution is the *cafetaleros*, the coffee producers. Coffee, whether destined for export or domestic consumption, is produced under a wider range of conditions than any other crop. Most coffee producers in Nicaragua are poor, have very small parcels, and use virtually no inputs other than family labor. There are also medium and large producers of more substantial means who use more sophisticated inputs and cultivation practices. The different types of coffee producers roughly correspond to the social classes existing in Nicaragua. Thus, studying coffee production not only reveals the importance of this crop for rural employment and income generation, but it also allows an examination of how the state has interacted with different classes. Specifically, it is possible to examine how certain interests of the state—generation and control of foreign exchange—have meshed with the self-interest of coffee producers—private capital accumulation.

Comparative research on the newly independent states of tropical Africa suggests several provocative propositions about what might be expected in Nicaragua, where the new regime is increasing its power considerably to achieve more equitable development.[1] Because of

1. See Stephen M. Gorman, "Power and Consolidation in the Nicaraguan Revolution," *Journal of Latin American Studies* 13 (May 1981), pp. 133–149; and Department

their historical development, the tropical states of Africa have more extensive state participation in the economy than is common in Latin America. This state participation is often introduced under the guise of establishing "African socialism." Rhetoric notwithstanding, however, the African regimes have tended to pursue policies that are adverse both to the interests of most farmers and, ultimately, to the welfare of the entire polity.

Their experience suggests that the decisive relationship between the state and small producers is the contradiction between the state's need for revenue and its avowed commitment to improve the welfare of small producers. Bates shows how regimes use state marketing agencies, which are publicly sanctioned monopsonies, and manipulate exchange rates to meet the needs of burgeoning bureaucracies and urban centers.[2] When governments reinvest resources in the agricultural sector, they do so to build support for the ruling elite. Consequently, the policies they pursue are not efficient. For example, although price policies with clear incentives are the most effective way of increasing production, governments prefer to invest in projects that are politically more useful. The consequences are twofold: a decrease in production and the subordination of peasants.[3]

The new Nicaraguan regime easily could be confronted with the same difficulties that have been experienced in tropical Africa. Somewhat paradoxically, achieving increased productivity will be easier for the large estates of the "bourgeoisie." First, these estates already produce high yields, and their accessibility facilitates assistance aimed at increasing production further. Second, their productivity and profitability facilitate the task of improving workers' wages. Improving workers' welfare is also potentially easier because the revolution—as interpreted by the FSLN—owes large producers, and the class they represent, nothing.

of Social Sciences UNAN, *Curso Sobre la Problemática Actual* (Managua: UNAN, 1982).

2. Robert H. Bates, *Markets and States in Tropical Africa: The Political Basis of Agricultural Policies* (Berkeley and Los Angeles: University of California Press, 1981). See also John F. Due, *Taxation and Economic Development in Tropical Africa* (Cambridge: MIT Press, 1963); John C. de Wilde, "Price Incentives and African Agricultural Development," in Robert H. Bates and Michael F. Lofchie, eds., *Agricultural Development in Africa* (New York: Praeger, 1980).

3. Goran Hyden, *Beyond Ujamaa in Tanzania: Underdevelopment and an Uncaptured Peasantry* (Berkeley and Los Angeles: University of California Press, 1980), pp. 9–25.

Given the size, wealth, and accessibility of large estates, the revolutionary government might be tempted to focus its attention disproportionately on large producers. Such a focus would undoubtedly raise political issues, namely, redistribution of wealth and income. A focus on large producers would risk giving short shrift to the real problem of the coffee industry in Nicaragua—the low yields of small producers. Current national production depends heavily on large producers, but major increments will depend more on small producers, whose problems could be aggravated if they are subjected—even indirectly—to policies intended to affect large producers by redistributing income away from them, such as through paying lower prices for coffee. Tension can be anticipated between the state's need for revenue and its avowed commitment to improving the welfare of small coffee producers, who cannot justifiably be sacrificed, given their class status.

Coffee Production in Nicaragua

Coffee production was the first source of capital accumulation in Nicaragua, and until 1950, it was the chief source of foreign exchange and employment.[4] Although cotton surpassed coffee as a source of foreign exchange, coffee production is still vitally important to the Nicaraguan economy. Although coffee production has not been as dynamic as other export crops since 1950, between 1960 and 1978 the area planted in coffee increased 49 percent, and production increased 148 percent.[5] That production increased at a much higher rate than the area under cultivation indicates that at least part of the coffee sector has adopted improved technology, resulting in higher yields.

Although the coffee industry represented only 6 percent of the gross national product in 1978, it provided 31 percent of export earnings.[6] The coffee industry is, of course, even more important to the rural areas. Nearly 21 percent of the area cultivated in Nicaragua is in coffee, and coffee provides 22 percent of agricultural employment

4. A discussion of the development of the Nicaraguan coffee industry and its impact on Nicaraguan society is presented in Jaime Wheelock, *Nicaragua: Imperialismo y Dictadura* (Havana: Editorial de Ciencias Sociales, 1980), pp. 13–48. See also Central Bank of Nicaragua, "Apuntes Sobre la Economía Cafetalera en Nicaragua" (Managua, 1978, Mimeographed).

5. International Fund for Agricultural Development (IFAD), "Informe de la Misión Especial de Programación a Nicaragua" (Rome, 1980, Mimeographed), p. ii.

6. Central American Institute of Business Administration (INCAE), "Nicaragua: Estudio de la Situación del Empleo, la Absorción de la Mano de Obra y Otros Aspectos en Fincas y Productores de Café y Algodón" (Managua, 1982, Mimeographed), p. 16.

throughout the year. During the harvest season, coffee provides 33 percent of employment.[7] These figures indicate the relative importance of coffee to Nicaragua's overwhelmingly rural economy. Coffee has been an important source of export earnings and of rural employment.

Despite the importance and growth of coffee production in Nicaragua, coffee has been the least progressive of the various agricultural export sectors. Most coffee producers have small holdings, limited financial resources, and scant technological know-how. Productivity is thus low. Before the revolution, the national average yield was ten quintals per manzana.[8] This compares with an average yield in Costa Rica of twenty-four quintals per manzana and twenty-two quintals per manzana in El Salvador during the same period.[9] Nicaragua's coffee trees tend to be considerably older than the optimum age for maximum productivity (five to fifteen years). According to some estimates, more than 60 percent of the coffee areas have plantations that range in age from thirty to sixty years.[10]

The generally low level of productivity in the Nicaraguan coffee industry obscures the existence of a wide range of yields. Coffee production is commmonly broken into three categories based on level of technology (traditional, semimodern, and modern), which correspond closely to the size of the producer's holding. Small producers use a traditional level of technology characterized by few inputs other than labor. Large holders use modern inputs and improved cultivation practices, allowing them to obtain yields up to six times those of traditional producers. This sector has largely accounted for the increase in coffee production in the last couple of decades. Medium-sized producers commonly use an intermediate level of technology. The relationship between the size of the production unit and the level of technology is detailed in Table 5.

Characteristics of Coffee Production

A recent INCAE study of coffee producers outlines the differences between the three kinds of coffee production.[11] There are an estimated twenty-seven thousand coffee producers in the country, and 85

7. Ibid.
8. José A. Buitrago, "Nicaragua and the Coffee Market" (M.A. thesis, London University, 1975), pp. 2–6.
9. Ibid.
10. Ibid.
11. INCAE, "Nicaragua."

Table 5   *Size of Coffee Holding and Level of Technology*

	Traditional (%)	Semimodern (%)	Modern (%)	Total (%)
Small	86.6	6.7	6.7	100
	(70.3)	(12.5)	(9.5)	
Medium	41.2	47.0	11.8	100
	(18.9)	(50.0)	(9.5)	
Large	14.8	22.2	63.0	100
	(10.8)	(37.5)	(81.0)	
Total	(100)	(100)	(100)	

SOURCE: Central American Institute of Business Administration (INCAE), "Nicaragua: Estudio de la Situación del Empleo, la Absorción de la Mano de Obra y Otros Aspectos en Fincas y Productores de Café y Algodón" (Managua, July 1982, Mimeographed).

percent are small producers (defined as having ten manzanas or less).[12] They are marginal farmers, relying mainly on family and, in some cases, local labor. Nearly all of them (99 percent) reside year-round on their farms, which are largely self-sufficient. Income figures are not available, but these farmers seem to have limited means. Around 40 percent of them had two years of schooling or less, and many were formerly wage laborers.[13] The INCAE survey found that 13 percent of small producers are women.[14]

The low level of technology small producers employ not only results in lower and less-productive employment but also lower yields, often as low as five quintals per manzana. At the national level, an estimated 63 percent of the area planted in the Pacific region and 50 percent of the area in the central and northern regions have yields of less than seven quintals per manzana. Compared with those from modern production, these yields are dismal.[15] Of course, production costs for small producers are low, enabling them to realize a gain nevertheless.

Medium-sized producers are classified as those with between ten

12. Ibid., p. 22.
13. Ibid., pp. 21–27.
14. Ibid., p. 22.
15. Buitrago, "Nicaragua and the Coffee Market," pp. 2–6.

and fifty manzanas of land in coffee. Most do not reside on their farms.[16] In general, medium-sized producers are of a different social class than small producers, with 24 percent having eleven or more years of education. Income and social mobility also tend to distinguish medium from small producers.

Most medium-sized growers use what is referred to as a semimodern level of technology in the cultivation of coffee. They use some inputs other than labor, especially fertilizer, and have adopted many improved cultivation practices. Consequently, their labor needs are much greater than those of small producers. The larger farms and the greater use of labor necessitate a year-round labor force as well as seasonal workers for the harvest. Permanent workers are often supported in part by giving them access to some land for basic grain cultivation.

In reality, the category of semimodern cultivation is an intermediate one that covers a wide range of different cultivation practices. As Table 5 shows, many medium-sized producers actually use a traditional level of technology. Those who do use an improved level do so in varying degrees. As they adopt improved cultivation practices, their costs rise. Of course, costs also depend on the efficiency with which they carry out cultivation practices. Greater yields offset higher costs. Although generalization is difficult, a yield of thirteen quintals is said to be common for semimodern coffee growers.

Large producers cultivate fifty manzanas or more of coffee. Seventy-four percent of them cultivate between fifty-one and two hundred manzanas of coffee.[17] However, some large farms are well over two hundred manzanas. As is the case with most medium-sized producers, most large producers (67 percent) do not reside on the farm. They tend to have more experience cultivating coffee than medium and small producers.

Sixty-three percent of the large producers use modern cultivation practices such as fertilizers, insecticides, and other improved practices. Most of the remaining large producers use a semimodern level of technology. The technology is labor-intensive—up to two hundred person-days a year are required per manzana. Costs are high, but yields are often five or six times those obtained by producers using traditional cultivation practices.

16. INCAE, "Nicaragua," pp. 27–31.
17. Ibid., pp. 31–37.

This description of coffee producers highlights their heterogeneity and underscores the large proportion of small producers with low yields. These two characteristics of Nicaraguan coffee production present a challenge to the revolutionary government. Its central tasks are to improve yields and raise workers' incomes. In a sense, coffee will be asked to continue making its historic contributions to the Nicaraguan economy. The presumed difference is that wealth will be more equitably distributed under the guidance of the state.

Government Policy Toward the Coffee Sector

Before the revolution, government efforts were limited to collecting taxes, negotiating with the International Coffee Organization (OIC) over export quotas, and controlling diseases. It did little to improve the low productivity of the Nicaraguan coffee sector; this was the coffee growers' task. Predictably, large growers were most able to improve their yields. Their superior level of education, generally better access to urban areas, greater ability to borrow from the banks, and disposition to take risks all facilitated technological innovation. Improving yields was more difficult for small producers.

Prices paid to producers depended primarily on the international price minus taxes and transportation charges. Nicaragua has traditionally produced about 2 percent of the world's coffee and thus has not affected world prices. In the short run, coffee prices have largely depended on Brazilian and Colombian production. Together, these two countries usually account for 45 percent of world coffee production. International prices have always fluctuated erratically.

Taxes on coffee in Nicaragua were increased when international prices were high. For example, in the 1977–78 season, when coffee prices were at an all-time high, producers received C$4.64 for every dollar of the international price. In 1978–79, when coffee prices were lower, the multiple was 6.17. (During this time, the exchange rate between cordobas and dollars was seven to one.) In practice, large growers were generally able to obtain a better price (for their larger production) than were small producers because they usually had greater access to roads; also their lesser dependence on private credit bound them less to a given buyer and price.

The triumph of the revolution has resulted in a much more extensive state role in the coffee industry. The seizure of the assets of Somoza

Table 6   *Ownership of Coffee Farms*

	Area (%)	Technology Level		
		Traditional (%)	Semimodern (%)	Modern (%)
State	15	13	16	17
Private sector	85	87	84	83
Total	100	100	100	100

SOURCE: Ministry of Agriculture and Agrarian Reform (MIDINRA), "Subsistema del Café" (Managua, 1982, Mimeographed).

and his collaborators gave the state ownership of nearly 14 percent of the land planted in coffee. The extent and structure of state ownership of coffee farms is outlined in Table 6. Three months after the revolution, the National Enterprise for Coffee (ENCAFE) was established as the only buyer and seller of coffee in Nicaragua. ENCAFE has set up sixty-five centers throughout the coffee-growing regions of Nicaragua to receive the coffee growers' harvests.[18] Given its monopsony position, ENCAFE is able to set unilaterally the prices paid to domestic producers. Equally important, the government has gained complete control of the foreign exchange earned by coffee. The government is paid in dollars and pays producers in cordobas.[19] Nearly 85 percent of Nicaraguan coffee is sold in Europe through the multinational Wappa Lloy Company.[20]

The new government has committed itself to renovating Nicaragua's coffee farms that have a low level of productivity because of their age and/or because they are affected by the disease roya. Rather than attempting to gradually raise the yields of farms with a low output through improved cultivation practices and increased use of fertilizers and herbicides, the government has decided to renovate farms completely. Once the renovation is finished, the farm is returned to the owner, who is given fifteen years to repay the government for the cost of renovation. The program is named CONARCA (National Commis-

18. *Barricada*, 17 August 1981.
19. Ibid.
20. Ibid.

Table 7   *Area in Coffee, 1979–81*
             (thousands of manzanas)

Technology Level	December 1979	December 1980	May 1981
Traditional	90	76–78[a]	76
Semimodern	20	20	20
Modern	30	30–35[b]	35[c]
Total	140	128–133	133

SOURCE: Ministry of Agriculture and Agrarian Reform (MIDINRA), "Subsistema del Café" (Managua, 1982, Mimeographed).

NOTE: No land was reported taken out of cultivation in 1982.

[a]90 minus 12 (affected by the CONARCA plan) equals 78 minus 2 (affected by the private and state sectors) equals 76.

[b]30 plus 3 (planted by the CONARCA plan) equals 33 plus 2 (planted by the private and state sectors).

[c]5 in development.

sion for Coffee Renovation). The area that has been affected is shown in Table 7.

The state has expressed a desire to provide technical assistance to all producers, but the requirements of managing state farms and implementing the CONARCA program have left few skilled personnel available for this task. Indeed, state farms suffer from a lack of trained and experienced personnel, a shortage that has been aggravated by the fact that farms in the CONARCA program have not been returned to their owners as quickly as planned. The government has been able to provide rudimentary technical assistance to some private coffee growers other than those involved in the CONARCA program, but so far with only limited impact.

While the government has been able to provide only limited technical assistance to private farms, private coffee growers have been affected by government policies in a wide range of ways. Indeed, some coffee growers maintain that the idea of a "private sector" in the coffee industry is a myth. The government, according to its own analyses, influences coffee production through numerous policy instruments: availability of land, availability and price of credit, availability and price of inputs, salaries and working conditions, and control of the price paid for coffee.[21] In practice, the government has not as yet developed a strategy for land use by the coffee sector.[22] But the other policy instruments have all affected coffee growers. The impact of government policies has been limited for the most part to changing the costs of production, revenues, and, consequently, net income. As an internal government document reports, "The state can regulate almost all of the prices within the [coffee] subsystem."[23] Of course, the smooth functioning of the system depends heavily—at least to date—on the initiative and responsiveness of private coffee growers. Comparing present production costs and income for the principal types of coffee producers with comparable figures before 1979 provides insights into how coffee growers have fared economically since the revolution. Of course, to determine which changes can be ascribed to certain government policies, we must control to the extent possible for exogenous changes. Because of the differences in coffee farms, we must consider small, medium, and large producers separately.

Production of Coffee

A bank report written during the 1978–79 agricultural season calculated production costs for the season at roughly C$500 a quintal using a semitechnical level of cultivation.[24] The cost figure is based on a projected yield of 10.5 quintals per manzana—the national average that year. Coffee growers interviewed regarded that cost figure as approximating the actual costs incurred in producing coffee that season at a semimodern level of cultivation. Hence, the figure can be used as a base for comparison with production costs in post-revolutionary Nicaragua.

Table 8 shows estimated production costs for 1982. A MIDINRA document reveals little disagreement on the production costs for the different technological levels of cultivation.[25] MIDINRA projected total costs for traditional and semimodern producers that fall within 2

21. Ministry of Agriculture and Agrarian Reform (MIDINRA), "Subsistema del Café" (Managua, 1982, Mimeographed), pp. 14–24.
22. Ibid., p. 7.
23. Ibid., p. 17.
24. National Bank of Nicaragua, "Costos de Producción" (Managua, 1978, Mimeographed).
25. MIDINRA, "Costos de Producción" (Managua, 1981, Mimeographed).

Table 8 *Production Costs per Manzana for Coffee, 1982 (in cordobas)*

	Level of Technology		
	Traditional	*Semimodern*	*Modern*
Labor			
(except harvest)	809.80	2,186.46	3,077.24
Fertilizers, chemicals	84.00	2,249.34	4,777.48
Equipment, tools	367.30	367.30	367.30
Services	—	—	255.00
Supervision and technical			
assistance	—	568.15	897.40
Harvest	2,887.00	6,904.80	14,385.00
Administration	210.00	454.00	664.00
Financial expenses	211.62	626.14	881.54
Miscellaneous	40.49	180.28	113.00
Total cost	4,610.21	13,536.47	25,417.96
Average yield	5 qq	12 qq	25 qq
Cost per quintal	922.04	1,128.04	1,016.72

SOURCE: Union of Nicaraguan Agricultural Producers (UPANIC), "Estudios Económicos" (Managua, 1983, Mimeographed).

percent of the Union of Nicaraguan Coffee Producers (UNICAFE) estimates. With respect to the modern producers, the government's figure was 13 percent below the private sector's.

A comparison of the production costs for semimodern producers in 1978–79 with corresponding figures for 1981–82 reveals an enormous increase in costs (total costs have doubled in three years). Wage increases have been responsible for a disproportionate share of cost increases. For example, the costs of harvesting coffee have more than tripled. Comparing prices paid to producers in 1979 with those for 1982 shows to what extent prices have offset production cost increases and provides a view of the changing incentives in the coffee industry. Controlling for changes in international prices provides an idea of the impact of domestic factors on the Nicaraguan coffee industry.

Tables 9 and 10 use production costs to calculate cost schedules, which can suggest coffee producers' incomes in 1978–79 (before the

Table 9   *Nominal Income of Coffee Producers*

	Cost/qq (C$)	International Price (U.S.$)	Domestic Price (C$)
1978–79			
Traditional			
Semimodern	500.20	161.70	997.20
Modern			
1981–82			
Traditional	922.04	123.40	1,040.00
Semimodern	1,128.00	123.40	1,040.00
Modern	1,016.72	123.40	1,040.00
Controlling for international price changes (assuming the same international price in 1982 as in 1978–79)			
Traditional	922.04	161.70	1,363.13
Semimodern	1,128.00	161.70	1,363.13
Modern	1,016.72	161.70	1,363.13

SOURCE: National Bank of Nicaragua, "Costos de Producción" (Managua, 1978, Mimeographed), and Union of Nicaraguan Agricultural Producers (UPANIC), "Estudios Económicos" (Managua, 1983, Mimeographed).

revolution) and in 1981–82 (after the revolution). Because production cost figures for 1978–79 are available only for semimodern producers, income can be calculated and compared only for this type of producer. Still, their income can serve as an indicator of the returns available to coffee producers in 1978–79. Income figures for 1981–82 are based on production costs as estimated by UNICAFE. Using government cost figures would not have resulted in significant changes, but it would have indicated less income to small traditional producers and greater income for large modern producers. Thus, the UNICAFE figures suggest less bias in the distribution of benefits than do the government's figures.

Real income for coffee producers has fallen precipitously. In 1978–79, a large profit was realized in coffee production, in part because of the high international price that year. In 1981–82, Nicaraguan coffee producers made little if any profit. Traditional producers realized the largest gain, but it was only a fourth of the gain realized by semimod-

Table 10   *Real Income of Coffee Producers*

	Ratio of Domestic to International Prices	Gain in C$	Prevailing Exchange Rate	Gain in U.S.$
1978–79				
Traditional				
Semimodern	6.17	447.00	7	63.86
Modern				
1981–82				
Traditional	8.43	117.96	32	3.69
Semimodern	8.43	(88.00)	32	(2.75)
Modern	8.43	23.78	32	.74
Controlling for international price changes (assuming the same international price in 1982 as in 1978–79)				
Traditional	8.43	441.09	32	13.78
Semimodern	8.43	235.13	32	7.35
Modern	8.43	346.41	32	10.83

ern producers in 1978–79. Modern producers realized a small gain, and semimodern producers lost an estimated C$88 per quintal. This drop in nominal income was exacerbated by the declining value of the cordoba.

Translating earnings into dollars provides a closer approximation of real income. While the present official rate was held at ten to one, the parallel legal rate was twenty-four to one during the harvest, and the black market rate was thirty-two to one. Coffee producers can exchange their cordobas for dollars only at thirty-two to one, and nearly all imported consumer goods are sold on the basis of that exchange rate. Nonimported goods have not increased in price as rapidly as imported products, but they have increased tremendously nonetheless.

Part of the decline in income can be traced to a drop in the international price of coffee. At the bottom of tables 9 and 10, an attempt is made to assess the decline in income, controlling for international price changes by considering the situation if the international price in 1982 had been the same as it was in 1978–79. The price of U.S.$161.70 is multiplied by the prevailing ratio between international and domestic prices, 8.43, to arrive at the hypothetical price for producers of C$1,363.13. Producers would, of course, have a larger income, but even in nominal terms, it would be much less than what they had earned in 1978–79. In real terms, the income gained would be only a small fraction of their previous income.

The government is primarily responsible for the loss of profit in coffee production. The monopsony of coffee allows it to set prices and control producers' incomes. Greatly overvaluing the cordoba allows the government to appear to pay the international price for coffee when it actually does not in real terms. Producers received C$6.17 for every dollar of the international price when the official exchange rate was seven to one. The present ratio between the international price and the domestic price is based on the official exchange rate minus taxes. In 1981–82, the ratio was 8.43—only slightly better than the 6.17 of 1978–79. Coffee producers—no matter what their size or class—have not been compensated for the cumulative effect of inflation since the revolution. In neighboring Costa Rica, producers are paid 4,000 colons per quintal. Although monetary comparisons between Central American countries are complicated, figuring according to the free market rate of exchange of 1.1 colons to the cordoba that prevailed for most of 1982, Costa Rican producers received nearly four times as much for their coffee as did Nicaraguan producers. While Costa Rican producers probably have higher nominal costs in general, they are not four times as great as the costs of Nicaraguan producers.

Differences in producers' costs and yields limit the exactness of tables 9 and 10, but the tables confirm what Nicaraguan coffee producers claim—that there is presently little incentive for them to produce coffee. The nature of coffee cultivation, however, limits their ability to respond to the lack of incentives by cutting back production. Coffee farms are in a sense fixed investments. A considerable amount of capital is needed to establish a coffee farm and to withstand the absence of revenues for the first three years. After this period, coffee trees will produce for many years if they are taken care of properly. A coffee producer cannot neglect his or her farm without jeopardizing future yields. The revolution has further increased the probable "cost" of neglecting to produce in any given year—any producer who does not produce is likely to have his or her farm confiscated.[26]

The "fixed investment" nature of coffee production and the threat

26. MIDINRA, *Marco Jurídico de la Reforma Agraria Nicaragüense* (Managua: MIDINRA, 1982), pp. 15–17.

of confiscation largely ensure that coffee production will continue even in the absence of financial rewards. This is especially true for small producers, who have few alternatives. As one small producer in Carazo put it: "If the price [of coffee] is not increased, coffee growers will lose the motivation they have to produce. The problem is that we have always supported ourselves from coffee cultivation, and if we do not work, we will not eat." While this suggests that many coffee growers will continue to produce coffee, there is no reason to expect that production will continue at the same level.

Theoretically, a drop in profit margins could be compensated by a higher yield, but seeking a higher yield inevitably involves greater costs and risks. Nicaraguan producers have sought the securer alternative of lowering costs. To a certain extent, the nature of coffee production encourages this strategy during periods of low financial returns and/or uncertainty. The use of inputs, such as fertilizers, and such cultivation practices as pruning can be reduced without a significant impact on yields the first couple of years.

Most Nicaraguan coffee producers have adopted this latter strategy, cutting back costs and adopting a wait-and-see attitude. Both the uncertainty concerning the direction of the revolution and the new government's credit policy have encouraged this strategy. During a period of great uncertainty, undertaking ambitious changes in the pursuit of higher yields—particularly if this necessitates large cash outlays—is not prudent. The government credit policy of providing 80 percent of estimated production costs encourages reducing costs by 20 percent so that all expenses are covered by borrowed money. The central reason for reducing seasonal costs remains the absence of a short-term financial incentive. The uncertainty about Nicaragua's political future and government credit policy have more of an impact on long-term investment decisions.

As pointed out earlier, there are considerable differences among coffee producers in Nicaragua. Also, despite the image many hold of the large coffee farm owned by an absentee landlord, most coffee producers are, in fact, small and of modest means. Coffee growers of all sizes—and hence of all classes—have been adversely affected by the loss of financial returns to coffee cultivation, as tables 9 and 10 demonstrate. Even more interesting is that coffee growers of all sizes have adopted the same strategy for coping with the loss of financial incentives to produce—that is, to keep producing but reduce costs even at the expense of declines in yields. A coffee grower in Carazo explained: "Even under the risk of a fall in the yield per manzana, we have adopted the strategy of maintaining production, but of reducing costs. These decisions are to protect us from having our land confiscated." Although a few producers have abandoned their farms altogether, cutting costs is the common strategy.

The government's rationale for complete state control of purchasing and marketing coffee is principally to ensure that foreign-exchange earnings will be used for the benefit of society at large. The argument is also made that the state will be able to free small producers from the control of exploitative middlemen. However, the extent to which the state monopsony has contributed to reducing the real income of all producers has created dissatisfaction among both small and large producers. A small coffee producer in Matagalpa, queried about how the revolution had affected him, replied, "The revolution has treated me badly; before, I could sell my coffee to anyone I liked." The INCAE survey of coffee producers found that small growers are more dissatisfied than large producers with government monopsony of coffee.[27] Part of the small producers' dissatisfaction stems from their living in remote areas (thus being farther from urban centers, where ENCAFE offices are located), but the central dissatisfaction is with ENCAFE pricing.[28]

Coffee producers' decisions to continue production so as to protect their investments have resulted in coffee maintaining its contribution to the economy. Indeed, with the drop of other exports, particularly cotton, coffee has provided an increased share of the foreign exchange earned by Nicaragua. But the strategy of reducing costs has led to a fall in yields, contributing to a decline in national production. The lack of proper care for coffee trees is also said to be partly responsible for the spread of the coffee disease roya.

The decrease in production and yields since the revolution can be seen in Table 11. High international prices in 1976 greatly strengthened a trend toward increased yields. The area planted in coffee was also increased, although several years elapsed before this increase contributed to national production. Yields declined during the revolution,

27. INCAE, "Nicaragua," p. 123.
28. Ibid. Dissatisfaction with government pricing is also reported in Institute for Economic and Social Research (INIES), "El Subsistema del Café en Nicaragua" (Managua, 1983, Mimeographed), p. 27.

Table 11   *Coffee Production in Nicaragua, 1972–82*

	Area Harvested (thousands of mz)	Yields (qq/mz)	Production (thousands of qq)	International Prices (U.S.$)
1972–73	118.6	6.43	762.5	50.3
1973–74	118.9	6.71	797.7	62.5
1974–75	119.0	7.50	890.7	65.8
1975–76	120.0	8.90	1,068.2	65.3
1976–77	126.9	9.50	1,205.6	142.6
1977–78	130.0	9.20	1,196.0	236.7
1978–79	135.0	10.48	1,415.0	161.7
1979–80	140.0	8.74	1,224.0	178.4
1980–81	132.0	9.73	1,284.9	120.1
1981–82	128.0	8.98	1,150.0	123.4

SOURCE: Union of Nicaraguan Agricultural Producers (UPANIC), "Estudios Económicos" (Managua, 1983, Mimeographed), and Ministry of Agriculture and Agrarian Reform (MIDINRA), "Subsistema del Café" (Managua, 1982, Mimeographed), verified with the Department of Economic Studies, Central Bank of Nicaragua.

recovered somewhat during 1980–81, and declined again in 1981–82. The CONARCA program has decreased the area harvested by twelve thousand manzanas in its effort to renovate unproductive coffee farms. Since the coffee farms selected for renovation were of low productivity, the decline in average national yield is actually somewhat greater than Table 11 suggests.

Determining the productivity and profitability of the state coffee farms, which account for 14 percent of the area planted in coffee in Nicaragua, is difficult. Private coffee growers are wont to belittle the state's efforts, but government officials often exaggerate the state's accomplishments. The sketchy evidence available suggests that the state coffee farms have been largely able to maintain production, but at a somewhat lower level of productivity than before they were confiscated and at a higher unit cost.[29]

The reasons for the decline in the yields of state farms are entirely different from those of the private sector. The maximization of output

29. MIDINRA, "Diagnóstico de la Situación de las Políticas Referidas a las Empresas del APP" (Managua, 1982, Mimeographed), pp. 27–29.

on state farms does not hinge on an adequate financial return to coffee cultivation or on a stable economic and political environment. State farms have suffered from two central problems: lack of capable administrators and lack of incentives. The latter is more serious with regard to holding down costs than to maximizing production.

The newspaper *El Nuevo Diario*, which is strongly aligned with the FSLN, published a remarkably frank letter addressing the difficulties in the state coffee farms.[30] The open letter was addressed to the minister of MIDINRA and signed by nearly one hundred peasants working on state coffee farms in the district of El Crucero. The peasants wrote: "The farms in this sector that are property of the people every day suffer losses because of the administrators in charge of the farms." They go on to say that the previous season's harvest had been poorly managed and that coffee farms are full of wild grass and weeds. They claim to have nothing personal against the present administrators of the coffee farms, observing only that they are unable to manage the farms successfully. Management of state coffee farms should improve as the state and its officials gain more experience.

The problem posed by a lack of incentives might prove more difficult to resolve. Although production goals can, and have been, established for different agricultural sectors and for individual enterprises, the problem is that—at least to date—it does not matter whether the goals are met. This is particularly true if production goals are unrealistic, as they often have been in the first three years of the revolution. Like other state enterprises, coffee farms receive 100 percent of their financial needs as determined by the enterprise, and there is insufficient control of costs. On coffee farms, the task is complicated by the difficulty of distinguishing between operating costs and investments.[31]

Investment in the Coffee Industry

The political and economic situation in Nicaragua since the revolution has scared private coffee growers. The Marxist-Leninist leanings of the National Directorate of the FSLN have led the private sector to question its future in the new Nicaragua. Furthermore, despite assurances that the economy will remain "mixed," coffee growers feel that the "rules of the game" have not been defined. They are

30. *El Nuevo Diario*, 11 March 1982.
31. MIDINRA, "Diagnóstico de la Situación," pp. 27–29.

not sure how they will be affected by the various state policy instruments in either the near or distant future. Especially troubling to coffee growers are the continued confiscations of land, particularly when they seem arbitrary.

As mentioned earlier, coffee production has been maintained in part because of the threat of confiscation for those farms that do not produce. However, confiscations and the political philosophy that is used to justify state actions have deterred coffee growers from renovating their coffee farms and from expanding the area planted in coffee.[32] Coffee growers interviewed knew of no one who had "invested" in coffee since the revolution. One of them replied that only a *loco* (idiot) would now invest in coffee.

In addition to the uncertainty within the private sector created by the political line of the FSLN, there is evidently no financial incentive to invest in coffee. The same forces that have dramatically reduced the incomes of established coffee farms have reduced the incentives to renovate old coffee farms and to bring new land into coffee production. A study by an economist working in the private sector estimates the costs of renovating a forty-manzana coffee farm and the expected returns, given three different assumptions about future average prices.[33] The assumptions involved in computing the costs and returns are conservative. Still, under only the most optimistic of the hypothetical conditions is there a positive return—and that is a yearly growth rate of 0.5 percent.

A coffee producer outside of Managua summarized the feelings of many coffee growers:

> The FSLN has not clarified its intentions; there is too much uncertainty to invest in coffee production, and besides there is no financial incentive to invest.

Another coffee producer voiced a similar sentiment:

> We think that it is better to wait and see what will happen; we believe it is better to be in debt [instead of committing one's own capital]; we do not know what the future of Nicaragua will be.

Even a government report acknowledges that coffee growers are pres-

32. INCAE, "Nicaragua," p. 234.

33. Union of Nicaraguan Agricultural Producers (UPANIC), "Costos de la Renovación del Café" (Managua, 1982, Mimeographed).

ently unwilling to commit their own capital to investment in coffee production.[34]

As previously mentioned, the government's CONARCA program for renovating unproductive coffee farms, particularly those affected by the disease roya, is probably the government's most ambitious investment in rural Nicaragua. It illustrates the potential and the problems of government investment in a revolutionary climate. The CONARCA program also deserves study because it deals primarily with small and medium-sized producers, who are supposed to benefit from the revolution. The average size of the coffee farm in the department of Carazo, where the program has been centered, is twenty manzanas.

When the program was first announced, coffee producers were enthusiastic. Everyone wanted to be rid of the fungus roya, and renovation would also upgrade the productivity of coffee farms. Coffee growers were promised a role in planning and implementing the renovation program and were quoted a figure of C$18,000 a manzana, to be repaid over fifteen years. However, once the program began, coffee growers had no opportunity to assist in its design and implementation or even the right to decide whether they wanted to participate.

The program proved to be fraught with mistakes. Instead of a step-by-step plan suggested by the growers, a massive scheme was undertaken. Land was taken out of cultivation faster than it could be replanted. In the first year, nine thousand manzanas were taken out of cultivation, but only three thousand of those were replanted. Thus, six thousand manzanas, or 4 percent of Nicaragua's coffee acreage, were needlessly taken out of cultivation. The loss in foregone employment and foreign-exchange earnings is considerable.

The replanting of coffee has often—but not always—been unsatisfactory. Difficulties arose from the lack of technical and managerial ability within CONARCA. In the first two years of the program, laborers often worked only a couple of hours a day because of a lack of supervision. Work was often sloppy, and there have also been charges of graft. Both coffee growers and CONARCA officials agree that after a couple of difficult years, CONARCA is finally attaining the necessary level of technical and managerial ability. Given the initial inexperience of CONARCA, errors should perhaps be expected in the first

34. MIDINRA, "La Política para los Productores Capitalistas" (Managua, 1982, Mimeographed), pp. 20 and 23.

couple of years, although many mistakes could probably have been avoided if coffee growers had been allowed to participate in program design and implementation.

Despite CONARCA's increased technical ability, coffee cultivators are bitterly opposed to the program on financial grounds. A coffee cultivator in Carazo summed up the attitude of many by saying the program was *un gran robo* (a big robbery). Coffee cultivators, who have no choice about participating in the program, are being charged C$33,000 per manzana. This cost is much higher than the initial figure of C$18,000 that the government quoted to producers when the program was being designed. According to producers, part of the high cost is due to CONARCA inefficiency. Coffee producers are especially irritated that the government does not pay them for the lumber it takes from their property during the renovation process.

An article in *Barricada*, the official government newspaper, reports that most of the renovated farms turned over to owners were in poor shape.[35] Many farms visited by reporters were said to be abandoned. The concern was that the lack of adequate care threatened the state's investment and future foreign-exchange earnings. The article did not attempt to explain why owners were not interested in cultivating their renovated farms. A coffee producer interviewed claimed that of the one hundred thirty coffee farms that have been renovated and turned back to their owners, only fifty are being managed conscientiously. The remaining eighty farms have been all but abandoned; only a minimum amount of work is done.

Conclusions

Reviewing the experience of coffee producers under the new Nicaraguan regime suggests the complexity of the FSLN's task of radically changing the prevailing economic and social order. Several of these complexities are worth highlighting. No simple dichotomy can be drawn between the "state" and "private" sectors, although, of course, there are obvious differences between the two. The new regime has such a wide range of policy instruments at its command that it decisively influences the private sector. Most of these policy instruments entail intervening in the major markets for the products affecting cof-

35. *Barricada*, 7 March 1982.

fee producers—the markets for the products they consume and sell and for land, labor, and capital. Recognizing the extent to which the state affects the private sector is important because it can explain the behavior of the sector. Each sector can aid or hinder the other, depending on the degree of complementarity, convergence, or contradiction in their respective goals.

That the state and the private sector can have conflicting interests is so obvious that it hardly needs to be stated. What is not always so clear is that this can be true even for those marginal sectors that a revolutionary regime proclaims itself committed to aiding. The marginal traditional coffee growers in Nicaragua have suffered from government policies as much as large modern coffee producers to whom the revolution owes nothing. In a penetrating study, Bates suggests that this is a common occurrence in tropical Africa where states have extensive authority.[36] He shows that governments intervene in agricultural markets to extract resources used to build organized support for the political elites and the politics they propound. All governments seek to maintain "solvency," and that imposes a need to garner resources—such as foreign exchange.[37] Rhetoric notwithstanding, the proclivity is always to obtain them wherever it is easiest. In the case of Nicaragua, where the state has increased its power, economic exigencies have led to a heavy "tax" (camouflaged as it may be by relying on manipulation of the exchange rate) on coffee producers—no matter what their class status.

The limited comparative work on revolutions in less-developed countries suggests that state power is inevitably significantly increased in the aftermath of a revolution.[38] Evidence also suggests that revolutionary regimes in the Third World inevitably pursue expansionary fiscal and monetary policies aimed at rapidly improving the welfare of lower classes.[39] Quite predictably, the expansion of the state sector and of its responsibilities quickly generates an acute need for resources—

36. Bates, *Markets and States in Tropical Africa*, pp. 6–7.

37. Norman Uphoff, "Political Considerations in Human Development," in Peter T. Knight, ed., *Implementing Programs of Human Development, World Bank Staff Working Paper No. 403* (Washington, D.C.: World Bank, 1980), p. 6.

38. See, for example, Susan Eckstein, *The Impact of Revolution: A Comparative Analysis of Mexico and Bolivia* (Beverly Hills, Calif.: Sage, 1976), pp. 11 and 19. Skocpol argues that this is a likely outcome of revolutions in general; see Theda Skocpol, *States and Social Revolutions* (Cambridge, England: Cambridge University Press, 1979), p. 285.

39. David Morawetz, "Economic Lessons from Some Small Socialist Developing Countries," *World Development* 8 (May-June 1980), pp. 357–358.

especially the foreign exchange so necessary to small states. How this demand is met is crucial. There are two dangers:

1. The rate of extraction is so high as to weaken incentives and ultimately undermines the nation's productive capacity.
2. Redistribution and taxation policies are indiscriminately applied to lower classes in the haste to generate resources.

Many African nations have suffered from a combination of the two factors. The evidence presented on Nicaraguan coffee producers shows that there is a real threat of the same phenomenon in post-revolutionary Nicaragua and suggests that it is likely to be a common problem confronting post-revolutionary regimes in the Third World.

Coffee production in the "new" Nicaragua also illustrates the limits of what "politics" can and cannot accomplish. Nationalization or redistributive policies cannot alone solve the principal problem plaguing the coffee sector in Nicaragua—low yields. State ownership of coffee farms introduces a whole set of managerial problems that—at least to date—make raising yields difficult. More important, the enormous number of coffee farms scattered throughout rural Nicaragua makes complete nationalization of the coffee sector unthinkable. Whether it likes it or not, the new regime depends on the private production of coffee, at least by the numerous small producers. Raising the low yields of small producers necessitates introducing them to improved cultivation practices, providing them with needed inputs, and, most important, making sure that it is in their perceived interest to adopt improved cultivation practices.

5

Peasant Subsistence Farmers
Food for the Cities

W HEN DISCUSSING agrarian reform, Nicaraguan government officials are disposed to concentrate on the distribution of land, the establishment of cooperatives, and other government policies directed at aiding peasants. However, agricultural producers—from marginal peasants to large producers—stress the importance of the relation between what they produce and what they consume. Because government agrarian reform policies are only a means to an end, supposedly toward improved welfare of peasants, the emphasis adopted here will be on the producers' concern—their real income. This approach will thus consider not only government policies directed toward peasants, but also other government policies that have affected their welfare, as well as general economic changes.

The thesis presented holds that the government's agrarian reform policy, which attempts to improve the living standards of the rural poor, is being overwhelmed by broader economic policies that act against the economic interest of rural producers, including the rural poor. Certainly, technical and social factors are important in understanding this phenomenon. Nicaraguan peasants have attitudes that are encountered frequently elsewhere; for example, peasants prefer private to cooperative ownership, and they resist efforts to create the latter.[1] But the real

1. On the difficulties of organizing the rural poor of developing countries, see Milton J. Esman and Norman T. Uphoff, *Local Organization and Rural Development: The*

problems stem from the political setting. The Sandinista movement derives its leadership and principal support from urban centers.[2] This has led to misperceptions of the agrarian problem (for example, over-stressing the previous forms of land tenure and presumed forms of exploitation and going for a quick solution through credit policies) to the neglect of more comprehensive and time-consuming strategies. More important, the urban base of the revolution has led the government to stress subsidizing consumption to the relative penalizing of producers, especially food producers. The need for subsidies to urban consumers, and the concomitant pressure on producers' incomes, has been exacerbated by the economic disruptions seemingly axiomatic to revolutionary change. Because Nicaragua is presently a mixed economy, peasants have responded rationally to price signals in a variety of ways: misusing subsidized credit for luxury purchases, selling produce to private middlemen, withholding produce from the market, and even withdrawing from production.[3]

Government Policy Toward Peasant Producers

The production of food crops has historically been largely left to marginal peasants employing backward technology. Small producers have traditionally grown 85 percent of the nation's beans and 90 percent of the maize (the two food staples). An exception to this pattern was rice, which increasingly was produced on large farms using modern agricultural technology. This bifurcated structure of Nicaraguan agriculture, begun with the introduction of coffee cultivation and perpetuated under the rule of the Somozas, prevented sustained development and had deplorable social consequences. During the reign of the Somozas, between 50 and 75 percent of the rural population had a resource base that provided only minimal subsistence.[4] This imbalance undoubtedly contributed to the fall of the Somoza regime.

State of the Art (Ithaca, N.Y.: Rural Development Committee, Center for International Studies, Cornell University, 1982).

   2. Robert H. Dix, "The Varieties of Revolution," *Comparative Politics* 15 (April 1983), pp. 287–290.

   3. The proclivity of peasants to adopt these kinds of strategies is outlined in James C. Scott, *Everyday Forms of Peasant Resistance* (New Haven, Conn.: Yale University Press, forthcoming).

   4. Philip Warnken, *The Agricultural Development of Nicaragua* (Columbia: University of Missouri Press, 1975), p. 44.

The new regime, through MIDINRA, has centered its efforts to improve the welfare of peasant producers on three policies: (1) better access to land at a lower cost, (2) formation of cooperatives, and (3) more credit. These three policies have often been tied together. In particular, access to credit and confiscated land has been linked to the formation of cooperatives. Cooperative members working confiscated land who demonstrate their organization's solvency can hope to have the land they work given to the cooperative under the agrarian reform. Unfortunately, the government has been able to provide small producers with only limited technological assistance that would enable them to raise yields, in part because of the great difficulties inherent in such an undertaking and in part because the government has seen small producers' problems as stemming primarily from the previous political order and not as technical in nature.

Most properties confiscated from the Somocistas were large modern commercial farms oriented toward export production. These were not broken up, as many peasants expected. Instead, they were converted into state farms to ensure state control of the foreign exchange they generate. However, some landless peasants have been given rent-free access to lands in the state sector if they form a production cooperative. In addition, decrees number 230 and number 263 reduce rental rates of arable lands. Previously, peasants had paid up to C$700 per manzana to cultivate basic grains. The maximum rent per manzana for basic grain cultivation is now fixed at C$100 (U.S.$10 at the official exchange rate). Landlords are required by law to rent their lands at the new rates to former tenants or sharecroppers. Furthermore, landlords are required to make their unused lands available to landless peasants at these rates. The rental decrees are thus meant both to give landless workers access to land and to reduce the cost of land to renters and sharecroppers.[5]

These measures have fallen far short of their goals in practice. In many areas, especially where land is scarce, the legal rate for renting land is not enforced. For example, in Masaya land is often rented for C$300 per manzana.[6] Private landholders have frequently resisted renting land to peasants altogether by planting sorghum or using their

5. Carmen Diana Deere and Peter Marchetti, "The Worker-Peasant Alliance in the First Year of the Nicaraguan Agrarian Reform," *Latin American Perspectives* 8 (Spring 1981), pp. 55–56.
6. Ministry of Agriculture and Agrarian Reform (MIDINRA), "Subsistema de Maíz y Frijol" (Managua, 1982, Mimeographed), p. 61.

land as pasture for a few animals. In other instances, they just claim they are going to put the land to one of these uses. State farms also have often resisted renting idle land to peasants.[7] The excuse offered is that the land will be worked by the state itself or that it is needed for pasture. The difficulties peasants encounter in renting land differ from area to area. Although land is more accessible than before the revolution, it is not as accessible as the government decrees intend, and access to land is still a problem for some peasants.

Well before the triumph of the revolution, the FSLN began encouraging peasants to form cooperatives. Agricultural communes, based on collective use of land and on collective work management, were first organized in the department of León. Following the victory of July 19, a widespread effort was made to organize cooperatives, the most advanced form being the Sandinista Agricultural Cooperatives (CAS). They are based on collective use of land, labor, and distribution of the surplus produced. Although only about fifty of these production cooperatives have actually been formed, the Sandinistas view the formation of production cooperatives by small property owners voluntarily pooling their land and other means of production as a long-term goal.[8]

Credit and service cooperatives (CCS) have been much more common. They are based on the organization of small- and medium-sized property owners to receive credit and technical assistance and to purchase inputs collectively. Cultivation is usually based on individual land parcels. Similar in organization to the CCS are the work collectives, which differ in that they are temporary—usually just for an agricultural season. The government claims there are approximately four thousand of these different types of cooperatives serving more than half of all peasant producers, or around sixty thousand peasants.[9] Because of the fluidity of the cooperatives and because at least some are little more than "paper cooperatives," evaluating the government's claim is difficult, but many knowledgeable observers believe the figures are overstated.

Cooperatives differ in many ways from one another, so only limited generalizations can be made about their functioning. However, it ap-

7. Ibid.
8. Deere and Marchetti, "The Worker-Peasant Alliance," pp. 55–56.
9. Center for the Study of Agrarian Reform (CIERA), *El Hambre en los Países del Tercer Mundo* (Managua: CIERA, 1983), p. 43.

pears that the more advanced the level of organization of the cooperative, the more likely it is to encounter problems. As is often the case with cooperatives, problems center on the division of work and the distribution of benefits. Other problems cited by peasants interviewed are the politicization of cooperatives and the amount of time taken up in political meetings. Many peasants just prefer the independence of working on their own, which is said to be *más tranquilo* (more tranquil).

Peasants who are interested in cooperatives frequently wish to reduce the size of their cooperative and to limit activities to obtaining and distributing government credit and agricultural inputs. Unfortunately, cooperatives of this nature provide limited benefits. In fact, a high MIDINRA official privately expressed the opinion that so far the cooperatives in Nicaragua have not reduced production costs or increased income.

The major incentive for peasants to join cooperatives has been the availability of credit. In fact, the new regime's greatest effort in aiding small producers has been in providing credit.[10] After the triumph of the revolution, peasants were strongly encouraged to join cooperatives so they could receive government credit. In some cases, they were told credit would not be available unless they joined a cooperative. In addition, financial incentives were offered: CAS members pay interest rates of 7 percent on agricultural loans, and CCS members pay 8 percent. Nonorganized small producers pay 11 percent for agricultural credit, while medium and large producers pay the prerevolutionary interest rate of 14 percent.[11]

Nicaraguan peasants traditionally had little access to credit; despite their great numbers, they received only about 7 percent of the agricultural credit dispensed in the previous regime. However, in 1980, the total amount of credit directed toward small and medium producers increased by over 600 percent.[12] The government went to such great lengths to distribute credit that even helicopters were pressed into action to reach isolated peasant communities.

10. See two lengthy CIERA reports, "Informe del Impacto del Crédito Rural Sobre el Nivel de Vida del Campesinado: Volumen 1" (Managua, 1982, Mimeographed) and "Informe del Impacto del Crédito Rural Sobre el Nivel de Vida del Campesinado: Informe Final" (Managua, 1982, Mimeographed).
11. Deere and Marchetti, "The Worker-Peasant Alliance," p. 57.
12. Ibid.

The massive infusion of credit into the countryside in 1980 did not have the intended consequence of increasing production and rural income. For the most part, the credit was not accompanied by access to technology that would have contributed to an increased yield. Even where it was accompanied by a new "technology package," principally in such Pacific departments as Masaya, results were disappointing due to high costs. Most of the production costs incurred in peasants' cultivation of basic grains are the imputed labor costs; few commercialized inputs are used. Hence, for most small producers, the credit received was just a windfall. A priest working in the agricultural frontier reported that upon receiving the credit—dispensed in cash— "peasants would go to the nearest *cantina* for a few beers and then go buy radios."

There were few controls on the dispensation and recuperation of credit, and less than 35 percent of the credit extended was repaid.[13] An especially serious problem was encountered in the agricultural frontier, where a lack of roads greatly impeded the sale of peasants' crops of maize and beans. Elsewhere rumors spread among peasants that there was no need to repay the loans. The government did little to persuade peasants to repay them, so the rumors proved to be true. Given the low repayment rate, the credit policy for small producers proved to be very expensive. Furthermore, the great inflow of cash into rural areas had the undesirable effect of stimulating inflation because for the most part it was not accompanied by increased agricultural output or an inflow of consumer goods. According to a MIDINRA official, there was also a suspicion in MIDINRA that the credit peasants received contributed to the labor shortage in the year's coffee harvest: having the cash meant there was not such a pressing financial need to work in the coffee harvest. As a special report of the International Fund for Agricultural Development (IFAD) acknowledges, the experience of 1980 showed that the mere dispersion of credit to poor peasants is unlikely to result in either a redistribution of income or a greater production of basic grains in either the short or long term.[14]

In 1981, the government quietly scaled back its credit program, particularly for maize cultivation, but credit has continued to be a keystone of the government's efforts to increase production of basic

13. CIERA, "Informe del Impacto del Crédito Rural: Volumen 1," p. 253.
14. International Fund for Agricultural Development (IFAD), "Informe de la Misión Especial de Programación a Nicaragua" (Rome, 1980, Mimeographed), p. 124.

grains. Because problems encountered in 1980 were never solved, credit has continued to be a largely ineffective policy instrument. By the fourth year of the revolution, the peasants' accumulated debt was so high that the government was forced to waive repayment.[15] According to an official of the National Development Bank, the amount waived is C\$370 million. Not surprisingly, there is a fear that canceling the peasants' debt will only undermine future efforts to improve their credit repayment rate.

The central means of institutionalizing the government's present policies toward peasants—increased access to land, formation of cooperatives, and credit—is the presentation of land titles to cooperatives. In the first two years, there was no legal distribution of land under the agrarian reform. At the end of 1981, the government began awarding to cooperatives that had demonstrated a certain solvency title to the land they were working. Since then, every month a few hundred families in cooperatives receive the land they have been working. The cooperatives usually have from twelve to twenty members. A single land title is awarded the cooperative, giving the equivalent of from five to twenty manzanas per member. Under the terms of the agrarian reform, the land may not be sold or distributed to heirs. By the fourth anniversary of the revolution, July 19, 1983, 693 cooperatives had received land titles. Another 645 titles had been awarded to individuals. A total of 305,030.6 manzanas had been awarded for the benefit of 20,236 families. The land distributed represents about 20 percent of Nicaragua's land under cultivation.[16]

Government influence on land tenure, which began with the seizure of Somoza's estates, was strengthened through the Agrarian Reform Law, announced in July of 1981.[17] Under the law, all idle, underutilized, or rented land on estates of over three hundred fifty hectares in the Pacific region and over seven hundred hectares in the rest of the country was subject to expropriation. Abandoned land was subject to confiscation regardless of size. The extent to and manner in which the government has altered land distribution as of the end of 1983 is displayed

15. *Barricada*, 20 July 1983.
16. Ibid., 22 December 1981, 18 January 1982, 7 February 1982; *El Nuevo Diario*, 18 July 1983.
17. For a compilation of decrees and laws surrounding the agrarian reform, see MIDINRA, *Marco Jurídico de la Reforma Agraria Nicaragüense* (Managua: MIDINRA, 1982).

Table 12   *Distribution of Agricultural Land, 1979 and 1983*

Property Ownership	Area in 1979 (thousands of mz)	Percentage of Agricultural Land 1979	Area in 1983 (thousands of mz)	Percentage of Agricultural Land 1983
Individual producers				
Greater than 500 mz	2,920	41	880	12
200–500 mz	980	14	730	10
50–200 mz	2,100	30	2,100	30
10–50 mz	910	13	1,000	14
Less than 10 mz	170	2	280	4
Production cooperatives			480	7
State farms			1,610	23
Total	7,080	100	7,080	100

SOURCE: Interviews with officials of the Ministry of Agricultural Development and Agrarian Reform (MIDINRA).

in Table 12. As the table makes clear, the new regime has decisively changed the concentration of land, although there is still a wide range in the size of landholdings. According to the government, 63 percent of the land that has been expropriated (beyond Somoza's assets) was idle or underutilized, 18 percent was rented to others, and the remaining 19 percent was abandoned.[18]

For the most part, the government has not been able to give small producers technological assistance that would enable them to raise yields. Although raising yields would contribute to increasing not only income but also national production, there are many difficulties. Agricultural education in Nicaragua has traditionally focused on the more remunerative export crops and concomitantly on modern technological agricultural practices. Other problems are the sheer number of small peasant producers, their concentration in isolated regions, the emigration of many skilled agricultural experts, the low wages paid technicians in the public sector, inadequate supervision, the unwillingness of many agricultural technicians to work in marginal rural areas, and, perhaps most important, the competing need of the state farms for

18. *Barricada*, 19 December 1983.

agricultural technicians. Overcoming these obstacles will be difficult.[19] However, because peasants using their existing technology can cultivate only a little more than three manzanas and because present yields are low, their technology must be improved.

The obstacles to improving peasants' technology are severe, but the government has not made much of an effort to tackle them, despite rhetoric to the contrary. The small producers' problems have been seen primarily as political—skewed land and credit distribution—rather than as technical. Yields could undoubtedly be raised somewhat by switching cultivation to more productive lands. Although this could be done in some cases, it does not seem practical for the majority of small producers. The real need is for an improved level of technology. Without a significant change in technology that will raise productivity, increased welfare for basic grain producers can be accomplished only by a revaluation of the worth of basic grains—in other words, through a redistribution of income within society.

Government policies seemingly have facilitated peasants' access to factors of production for growing basic grains, rather than influencing the cost of producing grains or the net income received from farming. But diverse changes have influenced the costs and returns for basic grains, the principal crops of peasants. Inflation since the revolution has been high, resulting in price instability. Also, the government now controls a large share of the market for basic grains and hence has a decisive impact on prices paid to producers. Given these changes, examining the shifts in production costs and selling prices and the relationship between prices of agricultural commodities and of consumer goods purchased by peasants is desirable. Doing so should provide an idea of the incentives to cultivate basic grains and of the changes in peasants' real incomes since the revolution, as well as illuminating changes in production.

Commercialization

The traditional system of commercialization of basic grains in Nicaragua depended almost exclusively on private market forces.[20]

19. MIDINRA, "Subsistema de Maíz y Frijol," pp. 64–68.
20. The following information on the commercialization of basic grains comes largely from a series of articles in *El Nuevo Diario* titled "Defensa del Consumidor," 1980–83.

The day after the triumph of the revolution in Nicaragua, the National Enterprise for Basic Foodstuffs (ENABAS) was created to distribute basic consumer goods at minimum prices as part of the new government's strategy to assist consumers. ENABAS is the principal organ responsible for guaranteeing the provision of foodstuffs essential for the population, as well as realizing programmed distribution of foodstuffs and defending the purchasing power of those with the lowest incomes.[21] ENABAS is authorized to export and import basic grains and other foodstuffs with the assistance of the Foreign Trade Ministry. More important, ENABAS acts as the discretional state buyer and seller of these products within the country.

Products commercialized by ENABAS are distributed in a variety of ways. The majority of the supermarkets that existed in Nicaragua before the revolution became partially or totally the property of the state. Administered by the Commercial Cooperative of the People (CORCOP) under the guidance of the Domestic Commerce Ministry (MICOIN), these stores are located in Managua and other urban areas. CORCOP cooperates with ENABAS in distributing basic goods at controlled prices. ENABAS has also used small private stores, government offices, and factories to distribute goods. Although ENABAS has attempted to reach out into the countryside, most of its beneficiaries are urban dwellers.

In the months following the July 1979 victory, food shortages and speculation led to increases of up to 500 percent over officially set prices. After this experience, the new government resolved to maintain low prices in basic foodstuffs and to avoid the sort of price increases that had previously occurred. Because this policy is based in part on the occasional importation of certain foodstuffs (especially basic grains) that are sold at lower prices and on the willingness of the state to absorb certain marketing costs instead of passing them on to consumers, the state has had to provide a subsidy. This subsidy has proved to be very large: the total 1980 government financial deficit, according to the plan of reconstruction, was to be C$900 million, of which the ENABAS subsidy represented 17 percent. This subsidy has increased every year. In the fourth year of the revolution, the subsidy to ENABAS was the largest government expenditure after defense.

21. Ministry of Planning (MIPLAN), *Programa Económico de Austeridad y Eficiencia 81* (Managua: MIPLAN, 1981), p.71.

Although basic grains—particularly maize and beans—are produced by the most marginal sector of Nicaragua, the peasants, the intent of ENABAS is clearly to aid consumers, not producers. Producers feel that the government-controlled prices are too low and do not provide an adequate remuneration for their efforts or an incentive to increase production. Peasants who cultivate basic grains maintain that because of the low prices, they are worse off than before the revolution. Furthermore, at least some peasants feel that the setting of prices for basic grains is the most consequential act of the new regime for producers of basic grains—more consequential than land reform, cooperative formation, credit distribution to small producers, or provision of technical assistance.

Evaluating the prices paid to producers is difficult, given that three exchange rates exist in Nicaragua. While the domestic prices of basic grains approximate international prices at the official exchange rate, domestic prices appear low on the basis of the other exchange rates: the legal parallel rate of C$28 to the dollar and the black market rate, which has risen steadily to eighty to one by the fourth year of the revolution. The terms of trade have clearly moved against peasant producers. Given the small size of Nicaragua and the weakness of its industrial sector, most consumer goods, including simple items purchased by peasants, must be imported. Although basic grains have been valued at the ten to one exchange rate, these consumer goods are often priced on the basis of a fifteen to one exchange rate the government uses, the twenty-eight to one legal, parallel exchange rate, or even the higher black market rate. Many imported goods purchased at the ten to one or fifteen to one exchange rates have been pushed up in price because of shortages and the knowledge that they probably can be replaced only at a much higher price. Domestically produced goods have also risen sharply because they use imported inputs and/or because of shortages.

Peasants, of course, are aware that their real incomes have declined. They are quick to point out that whereas in the past a certain quantity of maize or beans was adequate to purchase a particular commodity, now a greater amount is needed. The value of what they produce is measured not in nominal terms but in terms of consumption value. Consequently, financial incentives are measured the same way. Table 13 details price changes since the revolution for agricultural inputs (which are not always used), basic grain selling prices, and con-

Table 13   *Price Changes, 1977–78 and 1982–83*
            (prices in cordobas)

	Agricultural Season		Percentage Change
	1977–78	1982–83	
Production inputs			
100 lbs. low-grade fertilizer	18	120	667
100 lbs. high-grade fertilizer	30	180	600
Truck rental per day	50	300	600
Selling prices			
100 lbs. maize	55	130	236
100 lbs. beans	80	350	437
Consumer goods			
6 children's aspirin	3	3	0
Plantain	0.3	12	4,000
Pineapple	0.5	10	2,000
Beef	2	28	1,400
Pork	2	32	1,600
Socks	15	50	333
Shirt	45	300	667
Shoes	80	350	438
Dress	30	350	1,167
Batteries	1.2	10	833
Flashlight	30	130	433
Cot	150	700	467
Radio	200	1,200	600

SOURCE: Interviews in the departments of Masaya, Managua, and León.

sumer goods commonly purchased by peasants. Reliably measuring price changes under present circumstances is difficult, but the prices cited give an impression, and, perhaps equally important, one commonly offered by peasants. Table 13 suggests that profit margins have been squeezed and that there has been an even more serious deterioration in peasants' terms of trade. This is especially true for maize production.

The United Nations Research Institute for Social Development (UNRISD) has likewise noted pressure on peasants' real incomes.[22]

22. Solon Barraclough, *A Preliminary Analysis of the Nicaraguan Food System* (Geneva: United Nations Research Institute for Social Development, 1982), pp. 57–84.

Reliable, macrolevel inflation figures that might corroborate Table 13 are not available, however. For example, the 1983 IMF financial year-book reports inflation figures only for 1979 and 1980 (48 percent and 35 percent, respectively).[23] Also, inflation rates vary for different strata of society.

Peasants have been unable to influence the prices paid by ENABAS through the organization that supposedly represents their interests. The small and medium producers of basic grains are nominally organized with other agricultural producers of similar size in the Small and Medium Agricultural Producers of Nicaragua (UNAG), but its representativeness is questionable. Its central purpose appears to be to mobilize support for the FSLN, and it is dominated by Sandinistas. Many small producers of basic grains interviewed confessed to being unaware of its existence or to only having heard about it on the radio. Others maintained that the people running the organization are not even agricultural producers. This lack of representativeness and independence calls into question the organization's willingness to fight for the interests of basic grain producers when they do not coincide with those of the FSLN.[24]

Nevertheless, an outline of the organization's views contains a reference to the discontent over the government's control of basic grains.[25] Although the twelve-page report has neither been widely circulated nor influential in shaping policy decisions, what it says about the policy toward basic grains is noteworthy:

> One of the most serious problems we, the small producers of basic grains, suffer is the price that we are paid for our products. We ask to be included in the commission that determines the prices to contribute our ideas.[26]

The producers also ask for greater control over large private distributors of basic grains and "for control over ENABAS's buyers, many of whom are dishonest."[27] The government newspaper *Barricada* acknowledged the problem in a lengthy article on basic grains: one proposed recommendation was to "avoid pricing decisions that encour-

23. International Monetary Fund (IMF), *International Financial Statistics Yearbook 1983* (Washington, D.C.: IMF, 1983), p. 71.
24. Barraclough, *A Preliminary Analysis*, p. 67.
25. Small and Medium Agricultural Producers of Nicaragua (UNAG), *Plan de Lucha* (Managua: MIDINRA, 1981).
26. Ibid.
27. Ibid., p. 7.

age, as is presently the case, producers to purchase basic grains instead of growing them."[28]

Peasants can obtain somewhat higher prices by selling to private intermediaries instead of to ENABAS. Domestically produced corn (white) and beans are preferred over the imported corn (yellow) and beans (harder) often sold by ENABAS, and because the government rations these staples, there is a "private" market. However, the government increasingly pressures peasants into selling their harvests to the government, especially if they receive government assistance. In some localities, peasants caught selling their crops to private parties have their entire harvest confiscated without compensation.

Paradoxically, whereas peasants have been unable to persuade the government to pay adequately for the maize and beans they grow, large rice producers have been able to persuade the government to pay well for rice. It is generally acknowledged in the agricultural sector of Nicaragua that the price of maize is "terrible" and that the price of rice is "good." When asked why the price of rice is good in comparison with corn, a member of the irrigated-rice growers' association (a nongovernmental organization) replied that there are three reasons: (1) the large rice growers have lobbied the government for a good price, (2) the government is a large rice producer itself, and (3) rice is a potential export. More weight should be given to the first two explanations than to the third. Rice is a potential export, but so are maize and beans.

Production

Price incentives—or the lack of them—help explain the production of basic grains. On the whole, production has been lackluster, especially considering that over three hundred thousand manzanas have been turned over to peasants who have traditionally cultivated maize and beans. Table 14 outlines the areas cultivated, yields, and production of the four basic grains cultivated in Nicaragua—maize, beans, rice, and sorghum. Maize has been the biggest disappointment. Production is well below prerevolutionary levels, although it has recovered from the low reached during the insurrection.

Maize production would be even lower if the government had not begun to cultivate maize using modern technology on state farms and

28. *Barricada*, 10 October 1983.

Table 14   Production of Basic Grains by Agricultural Season,
1978–83

	1978–79	1979–80	1980–81	1981–82	1982–83
Area cultivated (thousands of mz)					
Maize	325.0	240.0	265.0	290.2	273.7
Beans	95.0	76.2	98.0	115.0	113.3
Rice	39.4	27.2	58.4	51.9	58.6
Sorghum	73.0	70.8	76.6	62.3	48.1
Yields (qq/mz)					
Maize	17.0	13.2	15.6	14.5	15.0
Beans	12.7	8.3	8.6	10.4	9.0
Rice	33.0	30.0	23.1	31.2	33.0
Sorghum	19.0	19.5	29.0	28.1	23.4
Production (thousands of qq)					
Maize	5,525.0	3,168.3	4,130.3	4,293.0	4,100.0
Beans	1,206.5	635.2	845.2	1,200.0	1,019.7
Rice	1,300.2	816.0	1,350.1	1,623.7	1,936.0
Sorghum	930.0	1,387.0	1,379.6	2,221.3	1,126.5

SOURCE: Union of Nicaraguan Agricultural Producers (UPANIC), "Estudios Económicos" (Managua, 1983, Mimeographed). Figures verified with the Department of Economic Studies, Central Bank of Nicaragua.

to coerce some large private cotton growers to do the same by withholding credit. Furthermore, production figures may actually be overstated; an economist working in Managua reports that maize production is only 40 percent of prerevolutionary levels. Also, the white corn grown in Nicaragua is rarely found in markets throughout the country. The lack of price incentive goes a long way toward explaining poor production levels; according to peasants, maize is not *rentable* (profitable). Some peasants report that they or their neighbors have discontinued cultivating maize or do so only to provide for their families' needs.

Bean production has been more successful, with production above prerevolutionary levels. Not surprisingly, peasants report that cultivating beans is more profitable than cultivating maize, although they feel

EMORY AND HENRY LIBRARY

the profit is nonetheless inadequate. As Table 14 shows, yields have not increased, attesting to the aforementioned lack of technical assistance to small producers.

Rice has been the success of the new regime, with production up significantly. Ironically, rice is not produced by recipients of the agrarian reform but by the government and large private farmers. (Production is about evenly divided between the two.) Increasing rice production has been easier than raising maize and bean production because of the relative modernization of this sector and the concentration of production. A question arises, however, whether the state has invested more in rice production since it became a principal producer.

Sorghum production has fallen, but yields have increased. In the aftermath of the revolution, many large cotton producers switched to sorghum production to cut their costs and labor needs. Because sorghum does not generate foreign exchange, the state has held down the price to discourage this practice. Unfortunately, the sorghum producers most affected have been small ones with low yields. Growing sorghum is now left to large producers with higher yields, but they too are slowly abandoning this crop.

In addition to problems of inadequate price incentives and lack of technical assistance, production in border areas is now threatened by fighting. Pressure from opponents of the regime also makes resolving some of the problems in the agrarian reform difficult. Resources are devoted to defense that might be committed to providing technical assistance to peasants. Also, as Commander Luís Carrión revealed in an illuminating speech, peasants are recruited by the counterrevolution, in part because of what Carrión termed "religious fanaticism," but also for economic reasons. This situation provides pressure to continue existing programs, such as credit provision, even if they are ineffective, because they have a constituency.[29]

Conclusions

Since assuming power, the FSLN has provided many peasants with access to confiscated land of the Somocistas and has reduced rents for peasants cultivating private land. Many service cooperatives, which have received government credit, have been formed. Although most cooperatives have not as yet received much technical assistance,

29. *El Nuevo Diario*, 19 June 1983.

the organization of many peasants into cooperatives should facilitate the provision of technical assistance in the future if the know-how, resources, and will are found. For cooperatives that demonstrate solvency, there is the hope of receiving legal title to the land they work. Many peasants have, in fact, already received land, and the government has announced that approximately one hundred thousand families will ultimately benefit from the agrarian reform.

The awarding of land titles to cooperatives in the departments of León and Chinandega has been especially significant. Competition for land has always been the most intense in these two northwestern departments. Beginning in the 1960s, large cotton growers seeking to expand began forcing peasants off the land they had traditionally cultivated. Year after year there were land invasions, which often ended in bloody confrontations between peasants and the national guard. Between 1964 and 1973, two hundred forty land invasions were reported in the region.[30] Thus, the awarding of land titles represents the culmination of two decades of land struggles by peasants in the area.

For many peasants, however, increased access to land and credit has been offset by higher prices for consumer goods and the government's unwillingness to pay higher prices for basic grains to protect peasants' purchasing power. Many peasants interviewed were aware that this was happening and complained that they have been worse off economically since the revolution. Not surprisingly, the Sandinistas' agrarian reform has lost support among peasants. A peasant in the department of Masaya summed up the attitude of many when he asked, "What good is a land reform if you have to sell your crops to the government for a low price?"

A UN study written in 1980 suggests that with the revolution, Nicaragua should be able to export significant quantities of basic grains.[31] There is a ready market for basic grains, which many Latin American and Caribbean countries import. Also, Latin Americans prefer the white corn grown in Nicaragua to the yellow corn grown in the United States.[32] Exporting basic grains would have several advantages: (1) it would boost production and income of peasants, who dominate basic

30. Orlando Nuñez, *El Somocismo y el Modelo Capitalista Agroexportador* (Managua: Dept. de Ciencias Sociales de la Universidad Nacional Autónoma de Nicaragua, 1981), p. 79.

31. United Nations Institute for Social Development, *Food Systems and Society: The Case of Nicaragua* (Geneva: United Nations Institute for Social Development, 1981), pp. 31–33.

32. Ibid.

grain production; (2) under present technology, basic grain production uses few imported inputs; (3) it would provide needed foreign exchange; and (4) it would lighten the dependence on traditional agricultural exports that necessitate many imported inputs and are produced by a class unsympathetic to the revolution.

By the fourth year of the revolution, the proposal seemed utopian. Nicaragua has not even been able to meet domestic needs. For the 1983–84 fiscal year, it has an estimated deficit of 3.1 million quintals of basic grains—maize, beans, and sorghum—equivalent to roughly 25 percent of national needs.[33] Scarce foreign exchange thus must be used to buy foodstuffs. Ironically, the purchases have largely been from the United States.

The Sandinistas' rhetoric suggests that the problems of peasants cultivating basic grains have been political—the usurpation of better lands by export crops, credit and resources flowing to the agroexport sector, and low prices for basic grains "to minimize the reproduction costs of labor." However, the experience of the last few years suggests that (1) reversing these resource allocations would be difficult, (2) many basic grain producers' problems are not political but technical, and (3) peasants' welfare is at least to some degree tied to the overall health of the national economy, including the agroexport sector.

This third point deserves elaboration. Predictably, the more remunerative agroexport sector is going to be controlled by an elite unsympathetic to an ambitious agrarian reform. If in a country dependent on agroexports there is a drop in the production of this sector, the resulting lack of foreign exchange is likely to slow the modernization of other agricultural sectors and push up the price of nonagricultural commodities—particularly, but not exclusively, imports. The government is likely to placate the politically influential urban sector by controlling prices where it can—domestically produced food. The resulting decline in the terms of trade for peasants decreases the real income for this marginal stratum of society. The Nicaraguan experience suggests that it is also likely to be a disincentive for increasing production and that it will, at least to some extent, offset specific government programs undertaken to increase production of foodstuffs.

33. *El Nuevo Diario*, 9 August 1983.

6

Rural Wage Laborers
Poor and Unorganized

W AGE LABOR has historically been impor-
tant to most rural Nicaraguans. As mentioned in the preceding chapter,
Nicaraguan peasant producers able to meet their household subsistence requirements entirely through their own agricultural production
constitute a mere 12.7 percent of the economically active agricultural
population. Only 7.5 percent of this portion of the agricultural population has stable employment. Landless workers without stable employment constitute 32 percent of the economically active agricultural
population. Most peasants in need of wage labor have access to only
seasonal labor, reflecting the almost complete dependence of the rural
economy on agriculture, which is inherently seasonal.[1]

The stratum of rural Nicaraguans dependent on seasonal employment as either a crucial means of support in conjunction with cultivation of basic grains or as a sole means of support has always been the
most marginal group in Nicaragua. Those with stable employment
were never much better off, unless, like mechanics, for example, they
possessed some special skill. Competition for stable employment kept
wages low. Examining how the status of rural labor has changed since
the insurrection provides insights into the ability of post-revolutionary
regimes to redress the inequities confronting the poorest and politi-

1. Figures are from Carmen Diana Deere and Peter Marchetti, "The Worker-Peasant Alliance in the First Year of the Nicaraguan Agrarian Reform," *Latin American Perspectives* 8 (Spring 1981), pp. 42–43.

cally weakest strata of society. In effect, the welfare of rural laborers is the "bottom line" for the new regime: FSLN efforts are all nominally undertaken to improve the poorest strata of the Nicaraguan population. Furthermore, the FSLN has sought to build its bastion of support in an alliance of laborers and peasants.[2]

Assessing the changes in wage laborers' welfare since the revolution is exceedingly difficult. Concomitantly, it is hard to assess the government policies that have been enacted, to measure their potential and problems, and to speculate about the effects of alternative policies open to the government. There has always been little published information on this social stratum, and although CIERA and MIDINRA are presently trying to remedy this situation, there is still a dearth of knowledge about the largest and poorest stratum of rural Nicaragua. A MIDINRA official, when asked about the economic composition and behavior of rural wage laborers, replied that this sector was *un gran misterio* (a great mystery). A more important reason why assessing the welfare of wage laborers is difficult is the fact that they are quite heterogeneous economically. This heterogeneity undoubtedly both explains in part the lack of published information on this sector and makes studies difficult.

Social anthropologists have increasingly recognized the economic complexity of the lower strata of less-developed countries, as well as the fact that much economic activity exhibits different characteristics from that encountered in developed countries. They developed the notion of an "informal sector" to apply to activities that normally fall outside the purview of standard economic analysis. Although the concept is not precise, informal sector activities are generally of a lesser scale than formal activities. A street vendor can be contrasted with a store owner. Informal sector activities are characterized as labor-intensive, family-organized, and noninstitutional.[3]

Research in Guatemala by another social anthropologist found that diversified income sources are common in rural areas.[4] In fact, diversification of income sources is the rule, not the exception, among rural inhabitants in Guatemala. Subsistence farmers with insufficient land

2. Ibid., pp. 40–73.
3. J. Douglas Uzzell, "Mixed Strategies and the Informal Sector: Three Faces of Reserve Labor," *Human Organization* 39 (Spring 1980), p. 41.
4. John J. Swetnam, "Disguised Employment and Development Policy in Peasant Economies," *Human Organization* 39 (Spring 1980), pp. 34–37.

to support their families migrate to work in the harvests of export crops. This migration is possible because the agricultural seasons of subsistence crops (maize and beans) are largely complementary to those of agricultural export crops (coffee and cotton). Cash crops may be added to subsistence crops during the dry season to provide additional income. Livestock also provides income.

Evidence suggests that the lower rural stratum of Nicaragua has income sources as diversified as those encountered elsewhere. The Guatemalan pattern of both cultivating subsistence crops and working as wage laborers in the harvest of export crops exists here, too, although the diversity of income sources is much broader. Nicaraguan rural households often have a number of income sources during any given year, many of them radically different from one another.

A striking example of this diversity comes from a woman interviewed at length in the populous department of Masaya: she raised ornamental plants in her backyard and sold them out of her house. She also raised small pigs, usually having between twelve and fifteen at any one time. She occasionally sold local handicrafts in the nearby city of Masaya. Her husband rented land on which he cultivated basic grains (maize, beans, and rice). He also picked coffee during the harvests. Thus, the household had a total of five different sources of income. Each individual activity was unable to support the household, but together they provided for the family.

Other examples come from rural inhabitants of the department of Boaco. One fellow interviewed had a full-time job in local government, made simple furniture to sell, and raised coffee seedlings in his backyard. Other individuals' cases are simpler, yet nonetheless similar: for example, one resident supported himself primarily by cultivating vegetables but supplemented his income by raising animals and occasionally putting up fences. A common practice in the area is to go to the agricultural frontier at the start of the rainy season and quickly plant maize and beans. People return to Boaco to resume their normal activities, leaving their fields completely untended until harvest. Yields are low, but the harvest helps them make ends meet.

These and countless other examples suggest that rural Nicaraguans commonly adopt mixed economic strategies that lead to work in the formal sector and the informal sector and to nonmarket work. Unstructured interviews suggest overwhelmingly that the reason for diversity of income sources is not choice but necessity. The diverse economic strategies result in an economically heterogeneous population, whose heterogeneity is accentuated by regional differences and the lack of factor (capital and labor) mobility.

In order to have a complete picture of the changes in rural welfare since the revolution, one would like an idea of income earned in the large informal sector in rural Nicaragua and an approximation of the income in kind generated by nonmarket activities. Unfortunately, this information is nearly impossible to obtain. No one knows, for example, just how many vendors there are in the rural villages of Nicaragua, let alone their incomes. A reliable approximation of rural employment and income would necessitate a large detailed survey. Furthermore, given the important regional differences in Nicaragua, such a survey would be generalizable only for the area in which it was carried out, unless extensive interviews were conducted in many departments. Such a survey would be costly and difficult to undertake at present. Aside from the obstacles engendered by recent political changes, there is the age-old aversion to specifying sources and amount of income.

A rough approximation of the changes in the welfare of the lower rural stratum of Nicaragua can be presented by combining comparisons of changes in the real salaries of the formal sector with peasants' impressions of changes in the informal sector. Interviews with peasants can also provide a view of changes in employment opportunities, working conditions, and political power. Assessing the impact of state enterprises is also necessary. This approach cannot provide anything more than an approximation of the welfare of those dependent on wage labor, but consistent trends can be delineated.

The Revolution and Rural Laborers

The struggle to overthrow Somoza and the triumph of the revolution deepened a sense of deprivation among peasants and created a sense of hope for a better future. These sentiments were widespread and not limited to those who participated in the struggle to oust the dictator or those organized into the Sandinista rural organization, the Association of Rural Workers (ATC). The FSLN had labored for years to convince peasants that they were being exploited and that a better future awaited them upon the triumph of the revolution. One of the popular FSLN slogans was "land for peasants."

Many Nicaraguans thought that after the revolution they would suddenly have everything they never had before, and they would no longer have to work. The Sandinistas, upon seizing power, confiscated only the assets of Somoza and his cronies. But peasants acting on their own seized many *fincas*, or farms, particularly those of absentee landlords. Other peasants demanded immediate wage increases and improvements in working conditions. Hours worked per day fell nearly everywhere, as did production. For example, a government official recounted that immediately after the revolution, peasants in the sugar cane farms of the department of Rivas worked only three hours a day, from six to nine in the morning.

The state was not immune from peasant pressure for immediate and radical changes. Indeed, the state was probably more affected than the private sector by the militancy the FSLN fostered. A miner in the town of Rosita recalled that after the nationalization of the gold mines in the area, "production fell enormously. When someone attempted to persuade the miners to work more, they cried out, '*No, no, Patria Libre.*' " (*Patria Libre* is a popular Sandinista slogan that means "free country.") Workers everywhere loosely interpreted the designation of state property as *Area Propiedad del Pueblo* (property of the people). In extreme cases, this interpretation led to the attitude, "I am the people, and I can use this article in my house, so I am going to take it home."

Initially, the new regime did not have the administrative ability to deal with the near-anarchy that broke out in many rural areas. Violence was for the most part avoided, but the regime was largely unable to stop nonfulfillment of labor obligations and politically inspired thievery and only partially able to control unauthorized land seizures. When the state was able to take a position, it nearly always sided with its political constituency—poor peasants—no matter what the issue or circumstance.

As the new regime consolidated itself, a loose set of goals was articulated for rural laborers. The collegiate leadership of the FSLN, and the lack of coordination between different ministries, makes pinpointing any definitive declaration of policy goals for the sector difficult, but such goals can be outlined as follows: (1) increased wages, (2) improved working conditions, (3) greater access to social services, especially education and health, and (4) increased political empowerment. The ministries of Education and Health undertook the provision of social services to neglected rural areas. The political participation of rural laborers was to be developed and channeled through the rural "mass organization," the ATC.

MIDINRA concurrently announced an ambitious agrarian reform to improve peasants' access to land. Success of the agrarian reform can aid rural laborers who are beneficiaries; however, rural labor will continue to be important for three reasons: (1) the decision to have highly productive farms confiscated by the state managed as collective farms, (2) the presence of private farms and enterprises, and (3) more important, Nicaragua's continued dependence on agricultural exports that require considerable labor input (such as cotton, coffee, sugar, and tobacco).

At the same time that state goals for rural laborers were being articulated, the new regime began to perceive the necessity of restoring the economy and to emphasize production instead of the redistribution of societal wealth. FSLN propaganda slowly but unequivocally switched from stressing the unnecessary poverty of most Nicaraguans to arguing the need for austerity and production. This change in orientation involved a shift from promoting labor militancy to stressing labor discipline. In concrete terms, this political line has resulted in salary austerity—in other words, the rejection of large salary increases. The explanation given to workers is simple: the economy was disrupted by the revolution; the state was left with the treasury empty; if the economy is not restored, there will not be the means to begin to satisfy the most elemental necessities of the people. Thus, there is no money to increase salaries and no margin to allow for lower production.[5]

The FSLN's austerity politics inevitably created a clash with workers, who had previously been lectured continuously that they deserved a better life and that such an improvement was within their reach. The strike at a plywood company three months after the triumph of the revolution is indicative of the pressures brought on by the FSLN's shift in politics.[6] The FSLN's handling of the strike reveals the delicate position in which it has been put in dealing with workers.

In late October 1979, seven hundred workers struck Plywood de Nicaragua. The company is administered by the government, although

5. This dilemma is discussed in Joseph Collins, *What Difference Could a Revolution Make?* (San Francisco: Institute for Food and Development Policy, 1982), pp. 69–78.

6. This account comes from Jorge G. Castañeda, *Contradicciones en la Revolución de Nicaragua* (Mexico City: Tiempo Extra Editores, 1980), pp. 49–50.

the state possesses only 32 percent of the shares in the company. The factory had not suffered any damage during the revolution, it was financially solvent, and 80 percent of its production is exported. As a generator of foreign exchange, it is one of the largest and most important factories in the country. The workers struck to demand a wage increase.

In the afternoon of the same day, Commanders of the Revolution Daniel Ortega and Víctor Tirado arrived at the factory to talk with the workers. The commanders responded to the workers' demands by saying: "The old systems of struggle are not appropriate in this historical moment. . . . If there exists a policy of restraining or limiting salaries, it is because the situation necessitates it. . . . The workers of Plywood should know that they are already in control." Given that the commanders' comments were widely disseminated—including four columns on the front page of the state newspaper *Barricada*—they can be considered an example of how FSLN leaders view workers' strikes for wage increases.

Conflict between workers seeking greater wages and power and the FSLN's politics of austerity and production has led the FSLN to increase its control over labor organizations. Sandinista labor organizations have increasingly been used to build support for the state instead of articulating the perceived interests of workers. Consequently, the unions, especially the ATC, have lost much of their support. Peasants interviewed reported that the ATC has virtually disappeared from many areas and that elsewhere it is little more than an arm of the state.

Independent trade unions have been pressured into affiliating with the Sandinista umbrella trade union, the Sandinista Workers' Federation (CST). The Sandinistas have been accused of using intimidation and strong-arm tactics to achieve this aim. A notable clash occurred July 8, 1981, when a delegation of banana workers affiliated with the Nicaraguan Workers' Federation (CTN) attempted to meet with the governing junta at the Casa de Gobierno. The delegation was seeking "the liberty of a union leader, respect for the right to unionize, a stop to repression, detention, and persecution of those peasants that did not wish to be affiliated with the CST."[7] The doors to the Casa de Gobierno were locked, and the delegation was attacked by members of the militia and the Sandinista trade union. A few injuries were reported. Al-

7. *La Prensa*, 9 July 1981.

though the intensity of this confrontation and the publicity it received have not been typical, conflict between the Sandinistas and independent trade unions has been all too common.

Despite Sandinista labor organizations' efforts to restore order in the nation's centers of work, labor agitation continued to be a serious problem well into the second year of the revolution. Workers seized factories, claiming that owners were "decapitalizing" or not meeting workers' demands. In rural areas, peasants seized land and farms they claimed were idle or abandoned. Strikes were a continuing problem. Although many workers' demands were undoubtedly justified, continued labor indiscipline was crippling the economy. Many owners of private farms and government officials administering state farms claimed that labor indiscipline was their most serious problem.

In an effort to deal decisively with the problem, the government outlawed all work stoppages, strikes, and seizures of centers of production on July 27, 1981.[8] The justification for the order was to "avoid having labor indiscipline make the economic situation more critical." The intention of the order was to "combat labor indiscipline and anarchy in production and centers of work."[9] The government proclaimed that the measure would be rigorously enforced. For the most part, the order was effective in halting strikes and seizures of factories and farms. The FSLN thus suppressed the very labor militancy it had fostered.

The net impact of the conflicting pressures on the state toward rural laborers—the commitment on the one hand to improve their welfare and, on the other hand, the exigencies of the economy that make the continued control and impoverishment of labor a structural necessity—can be assessed by comparing salary increases with increases in the cost of living and by examing laborers' perceptions of changes in their general welfare. Given the state's contradictory position toward rural laborers, it is important to examine which benefits have resulted from unorganized pressures on the part of workers and which improvements have been initiated by the regime and its organizations. Before evaluating the changes in the welfare of rural laborers, however, it is useful to compare salaries and working conditions in state farms and enterprises with those in the private sector to see how the welfare of

8. Ibid., 27 July 1981.
9. Ibid., 29 July 1981.

labor has been influenced by the tension between the state and the private sector. This comparison may also suggest insights into how labor might fare in an agricultural sector completely dominated by the state.

The State as an Employer

In certain respects, state farms are similar to those of the private sector. They are concentrated in the most productive regions of the country. Consequently, demand for labor is likewise geographically concentrated. An estimated 70 percent of the MIDINRA's permanent employees are in three well-defined regions: (1) the cotton-growing region of León and Chinandega, (2) the coffee zone of Matagalpa and Jinotega, and (3) the coffee zone of Managua-Carazo.[10] More important, as in the private sector, temporary workers make up more than 70 percent of the labor force.[11]

That state farms should be similar to private farms in their locations in the country's wealthiest regions and dependence on temporary labor is not surprising. Confiscated from the private sector, state farms came with an established mode of production that cannot quickly be changed. But the Sandinistas criticized the previous regime for not developing marginal areas and for leaving peasants without work for much of the year. Now that the Sandinistas are in authority, the challenge for them is to provide employment in marginal areas and to increase the amount of permanent employment offered to peasants.

Not surprisingly, in the aftermath of the revolution, peasants pressured state farms into increasing employment beyond what was necessary, both by taking on additional workers and by not discharging temporary workers. The new regime was sympathetic to these demands. One study suggests that employment on state rural enterprises increased 25 percent within two years of their being confiscated.[12] MIDINRA officials interviewed claimed to be unsure of the extent of increased employment but acknowledged it was significant.

In some cases, the increase in employment is due to an expansion in production; in other cases, it stems from the development of new activities. An interesting and promising example is the planting of tobacco

10. International Fund for Agricultural Development (IFAD), "Informe de la Misión Especial de Programación a Nicaragua" (Rome, 1980, Mimeographed), p. 92.
11. Ibid.
12. Ibid, p. 88.

by the sugar refinery enterprise Julio Buitrago. Workers tend the to-bacco principally while there is little work in the cane fields and at the sugar refinery. In some other refineries, workers have been employed in the construction activities designed to improve their living and working conditions.[13]

In most cases, though, the increase in employment does not seem to have been productively absorbed. Projects or activities to use the additional labor have not been developed. Most projects require skilled workers, who are not always available. Problems of worker productivity have been complicated by inadequate supervision and management. In many cases, these difficulties have disrupted the productivity of not only recently employed workers but also the pre-viously existing labor force.

The Reaction of Private Employers

With respect to labor, private farms see the state as a compet-itor and have sought to match or better state salaries in an attempt to attract and retain good workers. The decline in worker productivity and the atmosphere of labor militancy have frightened private employ-ers. Especially alarming are incidents where workers seize property. Although the government has outlawed unauthorized property sei-zures, many large agricultural producers fear that labor problems could lead to state confiscation. Consequently, many private employ-ers have sought to insulate their workers from the militancy of the revolution.

In addition to paying higher wages, many employers seek to avoid taking on new employees whom they do not know or trust. A seem-ingly docile worker may turn out to be a militant labor agitator. In gen-eral, having a few loyal, well-paid workers is considered better than having a large number of workers of average ability and little commit-ment to the interests of the employer, even if the enterprise is somewhat understaffed. Predictably, this strategy has contributed to the increase in unemployment in rural areas.

Many private employers also attempt to build strong patron-client relationships in order to secure the loyalty of existing workers. They

13. Ibid.

offer special privileges of one sort or another, the most important of which usually seems to be a loose form of social insurance (the patron assumes a willingness to provide for any emergency). At least some peasants find this enticing. For example, a few said they prefer working for a private farm because if someone in their family falls seriously ill, their patron will provide medical care and necessary medicine, something that, according to them, the state cannot be counted on to provide.

Many private employers seem to calculate carefully the wages and benefits they offer in order to compete effectively with the state in attracting good and loyal workers. For example, in northern Chontales, workers report that private employers need not pay more than the state because state farms in the area require a high degree of political involvement, including meeting attendance and occasional all-night guard duty. Having to participate in the political activities is seen as a disadvantage—not necessarily because peasants disagree with the political line, but because it is time-consuming. Although work is said to be easier on state farms, private employers are able to attract good workers without paying more than the state because they do not require them to participate in after-hours political activity.

In the area surrounding Bluefields, workers report that private employers pay more than the state. Work is said to be easier on state farms, and because the state is not as organized in Zelaya, workers are not required to participate in political activities. Consequently, private employers in the area pay higher wages to offset the advantage of easier work on state enterprises. Although there are undoubtedly many exceptions, state farms seem to have had a beneficial—if slight—effect on the salaries and working conditions of workers in the private sector.

However, state enterprises may also have had a moderating influence on the worker militancy that the insurrection ignited. Worker militancy at present seems only to lead to an enterprise becoming managed by the state. In the eyes of many rural Nicaraguans, working for the state is not appreciably better than working in the private sector, and many people prefer the latter. Moreover, the state is becoming increasingly sensitive to private producers' need for labor harmony. As a producer itself, the state is keenly aware of how labor indiscipline can disrupt production. Thus, state enterprises have contributed to weakening labor militancy in two distinct ways: (1) they have weak-

Table 15 Daily Wages for Agricultural Workers Compared to Consumer Price Indices, 1977–82, by Agricultural Season (prices in cordobas)

	1977–78	1978–79	1979–80	1980–81	1981–82
Total wage paid for those not receiving meals and lodging	20.73	20.73	30.73	40.44	40.00
Percent increase in wages (1978–79 base year)					
Current	—	0	48.2	31.6	0
Cumulative	—	0	48.2	95.1	95.2
Percent increase in consumer prices (1978–79 base year)					
Current	—	48	35.0	35.0	35.0
Cumulative	—	48	99.8	169.7	264.1
Percent gain (loss) in real income (1978–79 base year)					
Current	—	(34.4)	13.1	(2.6)	(26.6)
Cumulative	—	(34.4)	(25.8)	(22.7)	(46.9)

SOURCE: International Monetary Fund (IMF), *International Financial Statistics Yearbook 1982* (Washington, D.C.: IMF, 1982); Rolando D. Lacayo and Martha Lacayo de Arauz, eds., *Decretos-Leyes para Gobierno de un País a través de una Junta de Gobierno de Reconstrucción Nacional*, vols. 1–5 (Managua: Editorial Unión, 1979–82).

ened the perceived value of what can be accomplished through labor militancy, and (2) they have lessened state tolerance of labor militancy, thus raising the cost of labor agitation.

Changes in the Welfare of Rural Laborers

Table 15 compares salary increases with changes in consumer price indices to determine estimated net changes in real income from 1977 to 1982. Salary changes are based on official government decrees. Predictably, salaries are lower in more isolated and marginal areas. Employers often overlook benefits that according to law should be paid. Interviews with peasants suggest that this was the case before the insurrection and is still true in the aftermath of the revolution on both private and state farms. This qualification must not be ignored, but Table 15 nonetheless provides a general idea of salary and price changes since the revolution. The cumulative effect of inflation has been much greater than cumulative salary increases; real wages for agricultural workers have sharply declined since the revolution.

Peasants interviewed felt that their real wages had declined. Although the nominal wage increases that rural workers have received since July 19, 1979, have varied immensely, reflecting the diversity of wages paid, the net effect has been the same. At one extreme, workers in a salt enterprise outside León had seen their daily wages increase from C$35 before the revolution to C$39 after two and a half years of the Sandinista regime. Given the devastating inflation in the same period, their real incomes have fallen considerably. Ironically, since the triumph of the revolution, the plant has been managed by the state.

At the other extreme, a worker on a coconut and pineapple farm near Bluefields in the department of Zelaya has seen his daily wage increase from C$10 to C$30 during the same period—a threefold increase. Nevertheless, he maintains that he is worse off because prices have risen even faster than his wage. As an example, he claims that whereas he used to able to buy a shirt for C$30, now he has to pay C$150 or more. Almost all rural wage laborers have had wage increases between these two extremes, usually parallel to the raises outlined in Table 15. Despite differences in wage increases, nearly all rural workers have had their increases more than offset by inflation.[14] Wages for general agricultural laborers were not raised for the 1983–84 agricultural season, leading to an even further fall in income. Interviews with rural Nicaraguans in late 1983 suggest that inflation was accelerating, too (undoubtedly caused in part by the increased burden of defense against the counterrevolution).

Comparing wage increases for permanent employees with those for coffee and cotton harvesters reveals that the sector that has always been the poorest and most marginal—the coffee harvesters—has received the smallest cumulative wage increases. Furthermore, skilled laborers, such as tractor drivers, have received the largest wage increases of

14. A decline in the real incomes of rural low-income groups is likewise reported by Solon Barraclough, *A Preliminary Analysis of the Nicaraguan Food System* (Geneva: United Nations Research Institute for Social Development, 1982), p. 58.

all rural laborers. Thus, state-mandated wage increases for rural laborers have been regressive; that is to say, they have favored those who were relatively better off to begin with.

A further difficulty for rural laborers is that employment is harder to obtain. Reliable statistics on rural employment do not exist, but rural residents interviewed throughout Nicaragua agree that employment is harder to find, particularly in isolated and marginal areas. The weakening of the private sector has resulted in a significant loss of employment. The cotton-growing area is especially depressed because cotton production is well under half of what it was formerly.

To a certain extent, the state has offset the loss of employment by increasing both the size of the army and employment at state farms and enterprises. Nevertheless, given its limited ownership of the country's farms and enterprises, the state has trouble compensating fully for the loss of employment in the private sector. Furthermore, the state has encountered difficulties managing many enterprises and subsequently has had to close or reduce operations. This is especially true of the Atlantic coast fishing industry, but even some small enterprises have been affected. For example, the previously mentioned salt plant outside León formerly provided work for one hundred twenty laborers. A year after its confiscation, there was work for eighty; two years later, only fifty laborers were employed. Managerial difficulties made continued plant operation at the previous scale impossible. Although not all its enterprises have experienced such difficulties, the state has so far not been able to offset the loss of employment in the private sector.

The fall in real income for wage laborers and the greater difficulty in obtaining employment since the revolution have pushed many rural Nicaraguans into the "informal" sector or into nonmarket activities, especially subsistence agriculture. For example, in the southern part of Zelaya on the Atlantic coast, many heads of households formerly worked in the fishing industry, either on fishing vessels or in packing plants. The Sandinistas have to date been unable to manage the confiscated plants adequately; consequently, most of them have been closed, leaving hundreds without work. According to local residents, many of the people laid off have "gone to the bush," where they will practice subsistence farming until things improve.

Because most rural Nicaraguans are involved in agriculture, moving into informal or nonmarket agricultural activities is not difficult or necessarily much of a change. The change is likely to be more of degree than of kind. Wage labor just contributes less to the real income of the household (income being measured in terms of both monetary and in-kind income). For almost all Nicaraguans, relying more on informal activities does not even come close to compensating for the loss of wage income, but it provides a loose sort of safety net, especially when combined with kin assistance. Unfortunately, though not surprisingly, opportunities in the informal sector are inevitably tied to the health of the formal sector. When the formal sector is depressed, earning income in peripheral activities is more difficult.

Although most rural workers have not received an increase in real income since the revolution or had access to greater employment opportunities, some have experienced improvement in working conditions. Many rural laborers, especially harvest workers, receive their food from their employers, and its quality has always been a concern. The present government has mandated marked improvements in the diet of harvest workers—down to the amount of soup and cheese they are to receive per week. Continued complaints about food have been commonplace on both state and private farms, but worker pressure and government efforts have clearly improved the food provided to many rural workers.

The government has likewise attempted to improve rural workers' housing. Special attention has been paid to the most marginal sector— coffee and cotton harvesters. Better housing has been difficult and slow to obtain because of the costs involved; in fact, few rural workers have yet to see any improvements in the housing provided by employers. Still, some progress has been made. The government has constructed a number of housing projects for workers of large state enterprises, such as the sugar refineries in the department of Rivas. Some private cotton and coffee growers have been pressured into upgrading the housing they provide to employees.

The new regime has also legislated diverse changes to better the lot of rural workers. For example, employers must keep first-aid kits at centers of work. The norms for overtime pay have been specified. Cotton harvesters must be paid by employers if their work is interrupted by rain. These and similar benefits have all contributed to improving the welfare of such workers.

An additional change favoring workers has occurred in patron-worker relations, although it is intrinsically difficult to measure. Workers are more respected, and grave violations of their rights are much less flagrant than in the past. Nicaraguan workers are sensitive to what they regard as unjust dismissals, and dismissing workers arbitrarily is now usually difficult. Workers can petition the Ministry of Labor if they have grievances, and although its resources are limited, there is a good chance there will be an investigation.

Changes in patron-worker relations have been limited mostly to greater respect for workers; farm and enterprise administration has been carried out in the same managerial style as was previously practiced. There is no effective worker participation in management of state enterprises. Decisions are made by those in charge and are executed by workers. The rhetoric of the revolution occasionally refers to worker participation, but the reality has been different. As one worker in the nationalized mines observed, "They say that now there is no boss, but there is a boss."[15] The Sandinistas have found just managing state farms and enterprises in a conventional fashion more than enough of a chore. Presently, there is neither the time nor the resources to experiment with worker participation. Whether or not there is the inclination is an open question.

Surprisingly, the lack of worker participation does not seem to be a major issue among laborers, who seem much more interested in having adequate management than in playing a role in it. Worker complaints about management seem to center on the lack of technically capable administrators, and not on the absence of a role for themselves. Workers on state farms have written numerous open letters published in Nicaraguan newspapers complaining about the lack of technically and administratively competent managers. Such an attitude is common among workers.

The state has concentrated on providing public services, especially education and health care. Education has been criticized for being overly politicized, and efforts to improve health care have been hampered by shortages of resources, but the regime is clearly increasing the number of rural Nicaraguans who receive essential public services. Improvements in education and health care are by their nature long-term projects, and it is not yet possible to evaluate fully the success of the new regime's efforts. However, rural Nicaraguans clearly perceive

15. Center for the Study of Agrarian Reform (CIERA), *La Mosquitia en la Revolución* (Managua: CIERA, 1981), p. 58.

increases in public services as inadequate compensation for a deteriorating economy.

For rural laborers in Nicaragua—and probably everywhere else—the most important issue is access to employment and real income. What the new regime refers to as "social income"—access to government-provided social services—is seen as a separate issue. As an internal government document notes, government services can easily be seen not as part of workers' salaries but as an "obligation of the state." Evidence suggests that this is, in fact, the predominant attitude of workers.

Conclusions

The damage to the economy caused by the revolutionary process has clearly put the state in a difficult position vis-à-vis rural laborers. Expectations ignited by the FSLN and the revolution have been difficult to fulfill in the absence of prerevolutionary production levels. Workers themselves have contributed significantly to falls in production by cutting back on the length of their working days.[16] The state is put in the position of having to prod workers into increasing their production and to control labor demands that could contribute to drops in production. As an internal government document acknowledges, the state is also in conflict with workers for the wealth generated by the economy:

> Everything indicates that the most important relationship that can be established is that, all things being equal, a general increase in agricultural salaries implies a decline in the funds of accumulation available for increasing the productive base [of the economy], above all if it is not accompanied by an increase in productivity.[17]

Despite claims to the contrary, the FSLN has unfortunately been put in an adversary relationship with rural wage laborers. It has had to move from inciting worker militancy to promoting worker docility, from or-

16. This is also noted by Collins, *What Difference Could a Revolution Make?*, pp. 74–76.
17. Ministry of Agriculture and Agrarian Reform (MIDINRA), "La Política de Salarios, de Organización y de Normas del Trabajo" (Managua, 1982, Mimeographed), p. 6.

ganizing labor unions to controlling them, and from preaching "a better life for workers" to urging "austerity and efficiency."

Under the program of austerity and efficiency, workers are asked to make sacrifices that they increasingly resent. For example, during Easter week of 1982, workers were forbidden to take the customary week's holiday, and no bonuses were to be paid for working through the holiday week. Workers at Nicaragua's largest sugar refinery, San Antonio, normally work that week because it falls in the middle of the sugar cane harvest. But they have always been paid triple wages for the week and were upset at the loss of the extra income. Other workers accustomed to having the week off were also upset. A coffee producer in Carazo reported that after the announcement, he was approached by his workers wanting to know if they had to work that week. He told them, "I don't want to break the law, but I can't force you to work. You know what the law says." One of the workers yelled out, "*Ay vaya esa mierda!*" ("Oh, forget that shit!") No work was done on the farm that week.

The inability of the revolution to date to provide a better standard of living and the continuing call for sacrifices have made many rural Nicaraguans sharply critical of the Sandinistas. For example, peasants interviewed outside the Jinotega said they felt the Sandinistas were "working for themselves, and not for the people." More commonly, rural laborers are cynical, with the hope they had at the onset of the revolution dashed. When discussing their life since the revolution, peasants often make such comments as "*Estamos jodidos*" ("We are screwed"). The attitude of many toward the regime is summed up by such remarks, common throughout rural Nicaragua, as "*La misma mierda, solamente las moscas son diferente*" ("The same shit; only the flies are different") and "*Un hueso diferente, el mismo perro*" ("A different bone, the same dog"). More quaint—but equally scathing— was the comment of one peasant that the "new" Nicaragua is "the same monkey with a different tail." The disenchantment of the rural poor cannot by any means be equated with support for the counterrevolution, but it does complicate the already difficult task of improving the welfare of rural laborers.

7

Contradictions in Revolutionary Equality

N ICARAGUA paid a high price to oust So-
moza. The UN reports that forty-five thousand Nicaraguans died in the
insurrection. The UN Economic Commission for Latin America
(ECLA) estimates that national economic output dropped 6 percent in
1978 and another 24 percent in 1979. Thus, 1979 production levels fell
back to those of 1962. Somoza left a foreign debt of U.S.$1.64 billion,
said at the time to be the highest per capita debt in any Latin American
state. Furthermore, only U.S.$3.5 million was left in the state cof-
fers—hardly enough to pay for two days' worth of imports.[1]

Generous international assistance was quickly forthcoming from
countries as disparate as the United States, France, East Germany,
West Germany, the Soviet Union, Bulgaria, Libya, Cuba, Mexico, and
Venezuela. The foreign debt was renegotiated in terms said to be unprecedented in their generosity. Mexico and Venezuela provided all-
important petroleum imports on concessionary terms. Between mid
1979, when the new Nicaraguan government was formed, and early
1982, it received about U.S.$950 million in foreign credits and
U.S.$250 million in donations.[2] In 1983, Nicaragua received an addi-
tional U.S.$624 million in foreign credits and U.S.$76 million in do-

1. George Black, *Triumph of the People* (London: Zed Press, 1981), pp. 200–201.
2. Solon Barraclough, *A Preliminary Analysis of the Nicaraguan Food System* (Geneva: United Nations Research Institute for Social Development, 1982), p. 81.

nations.[3] Given the small size of the country, this outpouring of assistance is phenomenal. In the post-revolutionary era, the annual value of foreign assistance has actually exceeded the annual value of Nicaragua's exports.

Despite extensive foreign assistance, the Nicaraguan economy has floundered. Moreover, the future does not look promising. Gross domestic product (GDP) rose 8.9 percent in 1981 over the depressed level of 1980, but the GDP fell by 4.7 percent in 1982; no improvement was expected in 1983.[4] Public spending escalated rapidly after the Sandinistas assumed authority, rising from 21 percent of the GDP in 1980 to 31 percent in 1981. However, this spending has not been matched by greater tax receipts. In 1982, the government faced a shortfall of C$500 million in its administrative budget—a deficit that has since worsened.[5]

More important, the dollar value of exports has been only about half the value of imports since the new regime assumed power. The balance of trade shows no sign of improving, with the 1983 current account deficit standing at U.S.$500 million. A similar deficit is expected for the foreseeable future. Because Nicaragua is a small, underdeveloped, open economy without the option of self-sufficiency, this trade deficit is menacing. If imports and exports are added together, they equal 70 percent of the country's GDP.

For Nicaraguans, these unfavorable macroeconomic indicators mean a declining standard of living. Poor Nicaraguans interviewed between 1981 and 1983 report that their standard of living is either unchanged or has declined since 1979. Responses of those who were government employees or recipients of the agrarian reform and those who work in the private sector do not differ. Inflation, shortages, and rising unemployment are of paramount concern to Nicaraguans of all classes. As a result of economic difficulties, support for the revolution and the FSLN leadership has eroded, although some, especially urban youth, remain strongly committed to the revolution.

The incipient industrial sector was badly damaged during the insurrection; over 25 percent of Nicaragua's factories suffered damage to plant and inventory. Consequently, industrial recovery will be neces-

3. Marc Lindenberg, "Political Perspectives in Central America 1983/84" (Managua, 1983, Mimeographed).
4. Ibid.
5. Ibid.

sarily slowed by the need to rebuild or replace productive capacity. However, with the notable exception of a 25 percent reduction in cattle herd, the more important agricultural sector was only disrupted by the fighting. Hence, restoring agricultural production appeared not too difficult.

Committed to more than economic recovery, the new regime also seeks a radical restructuring of Nicaraguan society. As the economic plan for 1980 outlines: "We are setting out on a road to build not only a New Economy, but also a New Man."[6] By 1982, the task was outlined in more specific terms. As a popular government slogan put it, "Defend the revolution for the construction of socialism." Examining individual sectors within the economy suggests that it is this attempted radical transformation of Nicaragua, predicated on accentuated class struggle, that has complicated economic growth and development, and not simply the task of reconstruction, the world recession, or even the counterrevolutionary pressures that erupted into fighting beginning in December 1982.

Some of the first acts of the new government nationalized large segments of the economy. All the properties of the Somozas and their accomplices were immediately confiscated. In all, the measures covered 25 percent of industrial plants in Nicaragua and two million acres of agricultural property (or roughly 25 percent of cultivated land), most of it fully productive. Direct foreign investment in Nicaragua is far less significant than in many other developing countries, and the new regime's only move against foreign capital has been the decrees nationalizing natural resources, giving the state control over mining, fisheries, and forestry. In addition, the new government nationalized the banking and insurance systems—the latter because it was unable to cope with the needs of a war-ravished country and the former because of the role it had played in the corrupt economic system of the previous regime. Finally, the government assumed control over all exports, and thus the foreign exchange they generated. As a consequence of the nationalizations, the public sector contribution to the GDP rose from 15 percent in 1977 to 41 percent in 1980.[7]

6. National Secretary for Propaganda and Political Education, FSLN, *Programa de Reactivación Económica en Beneficio del Pueblo* (Managua: National Secretary for Propaganda and Political Education, FSLN, 1980), p. 31.

7. Black, *Triumph of the People*, pp. 210–211; Thomas W. Walker, *Nicaragua* (Boulder, Colo.: Westview Press, 1981), p. 59; Henri Weber, *Nicaragua: The Sandinista Revolution* (London: Verso Editions, 1981), pp. 61–62.

Export Generation and the Rural Poor

Although the seizure of Somocista assets gave the state direct management of 25 percent of the economy, the other 75 percent remained in the hands of the private sector. Control of banking and foreign trade, as well as the ability to rule simply by decree, has enabled the state to limit the earnings of the elite that dominated the agroexport sector, especially cotton, the linchpin of the economy. As it became clear that the state was committed, in the words of one producer, to the disappearance of this class, investment halted and production began to decline. The area cultivated in cotton has consistently been less than half of what it was before the revolution, leading to a precipitous drop in foreign-exchange earnings.

To prevent cotton production from collapsing completely, the state has had to make sufficient concessions to the large producers who dominate production. Generous credit has been made available; the state has held down wage increases for labor and even used its organizations to help producers obtain labor during the harvest season; and, most important, the state has provided special price concessions based on a fifteen to one exchange rate instead of the ten to one official exchange rate used for other agricultural producers. Government rhetoric suggests that, despite these concessions, large producers do not have a future in Nicaragua, but the concessions lead many producers to conclude that "there is money to be made in every tragedy" and to maintain existing production for the most part.

The contradictions in the state's policies toward large cotton producers are representative of the difficult position the state is in with regard to the entire agroexport sector. Table 16 details the volume per thousand quintals of Nicaragua's principal exports from the 1978–79 through the 1982–83 agricultural seasons. Exports have been depressed, especially cotton and beef. In its efforts to stimulate exports, the post-revolutionary regime has had to offer concessions to the traditional agroexport elite. Yet the same economic crisis has undermined the value of incentives because of the debasement of the national currency and because the state has been forced to increase taxes. As one cotton producer put it, "The state takes away with one hand the incentives that it gives with the other hand." Still, the traditional elite receives whatever concessions are to be had.

Concomitantly, the state allocates significant scarce resources, not

Table 16 Principal Exports by Agricultural Cycle, 1978–83
(volume per thousand qq)

	1978–79	1979–80	1980–81	1981–82	1982–83
Cotton	2,804	2,470	427	2,627	1,352
Coffee	1,188	1,204	1,000	1,132	1,011
Beef	749	783	450	209	320
Sugar	2,126	2,974	1,348	2,232	2,065

SOURCE: Interviews at the Ministry of Foreign Trade (MICE) and the Ministry of Agriculture and Agrarian Reform (MIDINRA).

to help marginal peasant producers, but to maintain and, it is hoped, stimulate production on the commercial farms it has expropriated. Priority is given to those enterprises that generate foreign exchange; indeed, nearly all state farms are devoted to agroexports. The relative strength of sugar production, for example, can be traced to the government's conclusion that sugar is the most efficient generator of foreign exchange in Nicaragua.[8] Production is roughly evenly divided between the state and the richest family in Nicaragua, the Pellas, who run Nicaragua's largest and most efficient sugar refinery. The state has concentrated resources in managing its sugar estates and refineries and is building, with the help of Cuba, a huge new refinery that will supposedly be the largest in Central America. The government's relationship with the Pellas family is clouded in secrecy, but the family is known to have immediate access to the highest-ranking government officials and is rumored to have received significant concessions.

The state's need for revenue, especially foreign exchange, has prompted it to expropriate nearly all the wealth generated by private production when the sector, or class, does not have the bargaining chip of withdrawing from production. Nicaragua's small coffee producers demonstrate that this is true even if the class status of the sector in question suggests it should benefit from the revolution. There are an estimated twenty-seven thousand coffee producers, and 85 percent of them are small marginal producers with yields only a fifth or sixth of

8. Ministry of Agriculture and Agrarian Reform (MIDINRA), "La Generación Neta de Divisas del Sector Agrícola y Agroindustrial de Exportación" (Managua, 1982, Mimeographed).

those of most large producers. Unlike cotton, coffee is a fixed investment; once plants begin to bear, they do so for years. Although one of
the rationales for the establishment of state monopsonies was to aid
small producers, small coffee producers report a marked deterioration
in their real incomes. The value of the national currency has fallen
precipitously; yet producers are paid for their crops on the basis of a
highly overrated exchange rate minus taxes. Because small coffee producers have a fixed investment and lack the resources to withdraw from
production, they can, as is commonly said, only hope for a better
future.

The modern commercial farms of the Somocistas were not broken
up and distributed to peasants as expected. Instead, the state assumed
management of them to ensure that they would continue to produce the
agroexports essential for the economy and that the state would receive
the wealth generated. However, land not part of modern commercial
farms and more recently confiscated land have been distributed to
peasants organized in cooperatives since the second year of the revolution. Around 20 percent of Nicaragua's cultivated land was redistributed by the fourth anniversary of the revolution, and land continues to
be redistributed to the landless.

Government policies directed at peasants have seemingly facilitated access to land for peasants rather than improving the net income
from agriculture. However, diverse changes have influenced the costs
and returns for the peasants' principal crops—basic grains. The scarcity of foreign exchange, stemming in large measure from the decreased
production by the bourgeoisie, has driven up the price of many goods,
particularly imported ones. The government has sought to compensate
by controlling the prices of many domestically produced commodities, especially food. Of course, food is grown by peasants, so low
food prices mean low incomes for them. Thus, the advantages to peasants of greater availability of land, made possible by the seizure of
large estates, are offset by the low prices paid them in order to protect
consumers suffering from shortages and inflation due to reduced agricultural exports. Peasants are well aware of the trade-off and resent
government price controls. Equally important, low prices for controlled basic grains have discouraged many peasants from growing
food except for their own families.

Ironically, the sector that has perhaps been called on to make the
greatest sacrifices for the consolidation of the revolution has been the

poorest—landless and near-landless agricultural workers. The FSLN labored for years to convince peasants that they were being exploited and that a better future awaited them when the revolution triumphed. Yet upon seizing authority, the FSLN switched its propaganda from stressing the unnecessary poverty of most Nicaraguans to the politics of austerity and production. This change in orientation involved a shift from promoting labor militancy to stressing labor discipline. Strikes have been outlawed, and labor unions are being pressured into joining a government-controlled umbrella organization. More important to laborers, the government's political line has resulted in salary limits and rejection of large salary increases demanded by expectant workers.

The deterioration of the Nicaraguan economy has been so extensive, and the reactivation of the economy so difficult, that the promised "liberation" of peasants and laborers has not been forthcoming. Instead, peasants suffer from low prices as the new regime hastily tries to protect urban consumers and from neglect as the state concentrates on managing large state farms that are judged more important for the reactivation of the economy. Laborers suffer from an enforced policy of austerity and efficiency. This situation has resulted not because the Sandinista ruling elite has desired it; there is no doubt that it would like to provide a better life for Nicaraguan peasants and laborers. Rather, the exigencies of the situation have made the continued impoverishment of peasants and laborers a structural necessity.

Economic Imperatives and Political Reality

The Nicaraguan case suggests that winning government concessions, such as the price of output, depends largely on economic strength and not the reverse, as revolutionary rhetoric would suggest. Furthermore, the state is not above putting its narrow self-interests above the welfare of weaker strata of society, as exemplified in the pricing policies for maize and rice. Peasants growing maize receive a "terrible" price; the large, capital-intensive rice producers receive a "good" price. The stated explanation is that the private rice producers have more clout with the government, and the government itself is a large rice producer. (State farms collaborate in the drive for a high price so they can show healthy financial statements.) Probably even more telling is the fact that the hated private cotton growers have received the most remunerative price incentives. Throughout the agricultural sector, prices for producers' output apparently depend not on their class status but on both the importance of the crop to the national economy and the elasticity of supply.

Economic dislocations and crises force post-revolutionary regimes to stimulate production in the quickest and most direct way possible, and that is usually through succumbing to the old way of doing things. The most ironic case is probably post-revolutionary Mozambique, with its continued economic ties to South Africa. The old order is thus appeased while the post-revolutionary regime seeks to dismantle it. What usually emerges is a web of contradictions with a verbiage that masks the opportunism of both revolutionary and reactionary actors. There is an economic logic, of course, to the state offering concessions to those who can best contribute to economic production. But this strategy is politically inconsistent with stated goals and, in fact, harkens back to the hated old order, where the strong were favored and the weak were ignored.

Despite the adroit consolidation of political power, efforts to efficiently manage the growing state sector, concessions made to the traditional elite still dominating production, and generous foreign assistance, the new Nicaraguan regime has not been able to provide a better life for poor Nicaraguans. Indeed, the situation is more problematic, as the regime openly acknowledges. In other words, the state has not only been unable to surrender control of the economy to the disadvantaged and the dispossessed, but it has also not been able to maintain relative levels of well-being. Stopgap measures, such as exchange rate controls, price controls, and rationing, have only moderated strong inflationary pressures precipitated by the combination of expansionary fiscal and monetary policies and the fall in output. The state thus not only is unable to award its supporters, and beneficiaries whom it would like to be supporters, but in fact also has to call for sacrifices.

Not surprisingly, post-revolutionary regime policies that change the economic fortunes of different classes have important political consequences. The responses of poor laborers and agricultural producers to Sandinista government policies show with piercing clarity that the political allegiance of classes is based on their perception of their well-being, not on ideological grounds. This is as true with lower classes as it is with upper classes. Ideology is important in shaping perceptions, but absolute and relative changes in material well-being are decisive in shaping allegiances.

Ironically, the rural poor can be an obstacle to radical structural change. Nicaraguan laborers seized the opportunity presented by the fall of the ancien régime to reduce their labor obligations. Peasants abused the government's generous credit program more consistently and blatantly than large landowners. Some peasants have been unwilling to produce food at government-set prices. In the post-revolutionary era, the faltering cooperation of the rural poor is not likely to receive immediate attention. Once noticed, it is not likely to be publicly discussed. It is an embarrassment that the supposed benefactors of the revolution prove to be as selfish as the economic elite of the old order. Rural laborers and peasants are unlikely by themselves ever to pose a political threat to a post-revolutionary regime, but they are likely to complicate its economic program.

Post-revolutionary leaders have to confront the expectations they raised during the insurrection period. The inevitable presence of counterrevolutionaries eager to exploit popular discontent makes this challenge all the more pressing. The temptation and danger is to resort to coercion, the *ultima ratio* of state power. Even such contemporary enthusiasts for revolutions as Paul Sweezy and Gérard Chaliand have commented on the "hardening" of Third World revolutions that initially enjoyed widespread popular support.[9] The economic difficulties and contradictions that confront post-revolutionary regimes, and the political pressures these economic problems bring, probably help explain why at least some post-revolutionary regimes become authoritarian.

Economic difficulties probably also help explain why some post-revolutionary regimes become dependent on international assistance, despite professed commitment to national autonomy and international nonalignment. Table 17 details the abrupt changes between 1981 and 1983 in the sources of Nicaragua's foreign loans, credits, and donations. A similar pattern has been reported in Angola and Mozambique. In Mozambique, the output of both food and export crops has fallen. The combined impact is that, at a time when Mozambique has become less able to feed its population, it has also become less and less able to pay for the increasing quantities of food it has to import.[10] Mozambique has sought economic relief from the socialist bloc. Although the

9. Paul M. Sweezy, *Post-Revolutionary Society* (New York: Monthly Review Press, 1980); Gérard Chaliand, *Revolution in the Third World* (New York: Penguin Books, 1978).

10. Michael S. Radu, "Mozambique: Nonalignment or New Dependence?" *Current History* 83 (March 1984), p. 104.

Table 17   *International Loans and Donations, 1981 and 1983 (millions of dollars)*

	1981		1983	
	U.S.$	%	U.S.$	%
Loans				
Multilateral	302	45	45	6
Bilateral				
Socialist	7		227	
Nonsocialist	33		296	
U.S. and Canada	123		15	
Subtotal	163	24	538	72
Credit lines				
Socialist	41		36	
Nonsocialist	98		45	
Subtotal	139	21	81	11
Total loans	602		624	
Donations				
Socialist	16		33	
Nonsocialist	45		35	
International organizations			8	
Subtotal	61	10	76	11
Total loans and donations	663	100	740	100
Socialist	64	10	296	40

SOURCE: Interviews at the Ministry of Foreign Trade (MICE) and the Ministry of Planning (MIPLAN).

desire to seek international assistance from wherever it is available is understandable, this strategy can result in a weak post-revolutionary regime becoming a pawn in the East-West conflict because of great-power opportunism and paranoia.

It is too early to judge the Nicaraguan Revolution, to pass judgment on its successes and failures. The emergence of a strong counterrevolution, made possible by U.S. aid, has lately engulfed Nicaragua, overshadowing efforts at broad-based economic development. The damage inflicted by the counterrevolution will need to be studied and appreciated. However, continuing efforts to understand Nicaragua's metamorphosis should not neglect analyzing the internal dynamics of revolution in a small developing country. Attempts at such analysis, such as this work, reveal Mao's wisdom when he wrote, as the People's Liberation Army was about to win its final victories in March 1949: "The Chinese revolution is great, but the road after the revolution will be longer, the work greater and more arduous."[11] Mao's admonition holds for every contemporary revolution.

11. Mao Tse-tung, *Selected Works*, vol. 4, p. 374, quoted in Sweezy, *Post-Revolutionary Society*, p. 53.

Bibliography

Amnesty International. *The Republic of Nicaragua: An Amnesty International Report*. USA: Amnesty International Publications, 1977.

Ascher, William. *Scheming for the Poor*. Cambridge: Harvard University Press, 1984.

Banks, Arthur. *Economic Handbook of the World: 1981*. New York: McGraw-Hill, 1981.

Barraclough, Solon. *A Preliminary Analysis of the Nicaraguan Food System*. Geneva: United Nations Research Institute for Social Development, 1982.

———. "Report of the IFAD Special Programming Mission to Nicaragua." Managua, 1980. Mimeographed.

Bates, Robert H. *Markets and States in Tropical Africa: The Political Basis of Agricultural Policies*. Berkeley and Los Angeles: University of California Press, 1981.

Belli, Pedro. "An Inquiry Concerning the Growth of Cotton Farming in Nicaragua." Ph.D. dissertation, University of California, Berkeley, 1968.

Black, George. *Triumph of the People*. London: Zed Press, 1981.

Booth, John A. *The End and the Beginning: The Nicaraguan Revolution*. Boulder, Colo.: Westview Press, 1982.

Brinton, Crane. *The Anatomy of Revolution*. New York: Vintage Books, 1965.

Buitrago, José A. "Nicaragua and the Coffee Market." M.A. thesis, London University, 1975.

Burbach, R., and Draiman, T. "Nicaragua's Revolution." *NACLA* (North American Council on Latin America) 24 (May-June 1980): 2–35.

Castañeda, Jorge G. *Nicaragua: Contradicciones en la Revolución*. Mexico City: Tiempo Extra Editores, 1980.

Center for the Study of Agrarian Reform (CIERA). *El Hambre en los Países del Tercer Mundo*. Managua: CIERA, 1983.

―――. "Informe del Impacto del Crédito Rural Sobre el Nivel de Vida del Campesinado: Volumen 1." Managua, 1982. Mimeographed.

―――. "Informe del Impacto del Crédito Rural Sobre el Nivel de Vida del Campesinado: Informe Final." Managua, 1982. Mimeographed.

―――. *La Mosquitia en la Revolución.* Managua: CIERA, 1981.

―――. "Significación de la reforma agraria." Managua, 1980. Mimeographed.

Central American Institute of Business Administration (INCAE). "Nicaragua: Estudio de la Situación del Empleo, la Absorción de la Mano de Obra y Otros Aspectos en Fincas y Productores de Café y Algodón." Managua, July 1982. Mimeographed.

Central Bank of Nicaragua. *Análisis Sobre las Perspectivas Algodoneras en Nicaragua.* Managua: Central Bank of Nicaragua, 1978.

―――. "Apuntes Sobre la Economía Cafetalera en Nicaragua." Managua, 1978. Mimeographed.

―――. *Informe Anual 1978.* Managua: Central Bank of Nicaragua, 1980.

Chaliand, Gérard. *Revolution in the Third World.* New York: Penguin Books, 1978.

Collins, Joseph. *What Difference Could a Revolution Make?* San Francisco: Institute for Food and Development Policy, 1982.

Davidow, Jeffrey. *Dealing with International Crisis: Lessons from Zimbabwe.* Occasional Paper 34. Musatine, Iowa: Stanley Foundation, 1983.

Deere, Carmen Diana, and Marchetti, Peter. "The Worker-Peasant Alliance in the First Year of the Nicaraguan Agrarian Reform." *Latin American Perspectives* 8 (Spring 1981): 40–73.

Dennis, Philip A. "The Costeños and the Revolution in Nicaragua." *Journal of Interamerican Studies and World Affairs* 23 (August 1981): 271–296.

Department of Social Sciences UNAN. *Curso Sobre la Problemática Actual.* Managua: UNAN, 1980.

de Wilde, John C. "Price Incentives and African Agricultural Development." In *Agricultural Development in Africa,* edited by Robert H. Bates and Michael F. Lofchie, pp. 44–66. New York: Praeger, 1980.

Dix, Robert H. "The Varieties of Revolution." *Comparative Politics* 15 (April 1983): 281–294.

Due, John F. *Taxation and Economic Development in Tropical Africa.* Cambridge: MIT Press, 1963.

Dunn, John. *Modern Revolutions.* Cambridge, England: Cambridge University Press, 1972.

Eckstein, Susan. *The Impact of Revolution: A Comparative Analysis of Mexico and Bolivia.* Beverly Hills, Calif.: Sage, 1976.

Esman, Milton J., and Uphoff, Norman T. *Local Organization and Rural Development: The State of the Art*. Ithaca, N.Y.: Rural Development Committee, Center for International Studies, Cornell University, 1982.

Gilbert, Dennis. "The Bourgeoisie in the Nicaraguan Revolution." Paper presented at the South Eastern Conference on Latin American Studies, San Juan, Puerto Rico, April 1983.

Gomez, Walter. "Bolivia: Problems of a Pre- and Post-Revolutionary Export Economy." *Journal of Developing Areas* 10 (July 1976): 461–483.

Gorman, Stephen M. "Power and Consolidation in the Nicaraguan Revolution." *Journal of Latin American Studies* 13 (May 1981): 133–149.

Hamilton, Nora. *The Limits of State Autonomy: Post-Revolutionary Mexico*. Princeton, N.J.: Princeton University Press, 1982.

Handelman, Howard. "Peasants, Landlords and Bureaucrats: The Politics of Agrarian Reform in Peru." In *The Politics of Agrarian Change in Asia and Latin America*, edited by Howard Handelman, pp. 103–125. Bloomington: Indiana University Press, 1981.

Hyden, Goran. *Beyond Ujamaa in Tanzania: Underdevelopment and an Uncaptured Peasantry*. Berkeley and Los Angeles: University of California Press, 1980.

Inforpress, 1981.

Institute for Economic and Social Research (INIES). "El Subsistema del Café en Nicaragua." Managua, 1983. Mimeographed.

International Fund for Agricultural Development (IFAD). "Informe de la Misión Especial de Programación a Nicaragua." Rome, 1980. Mimeographed.

International Monetary Fund (IMF). *International Financial Statistics Yearbook, 1983*. Washington, D.C.: IMF, 1983.

Isaacman, Allen, and Isaacman, Barbara. *Mozambique: From Colonialism to Revolution, 1900–1982*. Boulder, Colo.: Westview Press, 1983.

Jorge, Antonio. "Economic Decision-Making in Cuba: The Transition from Capitalism to Communism." *Journal of Interamerican Studies and World Affairs* 25 (May 1983): 251–267.

Kaimowitz, David, and Thome, Joseph. *Nicaragua's Agrarian Reform: The First Year (1979–1980)*. Madison: Land Tenure Center, University of Wisconsin-Madison, 1981.

Lacayo, Rolando D., and Lacayo de Arauz, Martha, eds. *Decretos-Leyes para Gobierno de un País a través de una Junta de Gobierno de Reconstrucción Nacional*. 5 vols. Managua: Editorial Unión, 1979–82.

Latin American Bureau. *Nicaragua*. London: Latin American Bureau, 1980.

Latin American Weekly Report.

Lindenberg, Marc. "Political Perspectives in Central America 1983/84." Managua, 1983. Mimeographed.

MacEwan, Arthur. *Revolution and Economic Development in Cuba*. New York: St. Martin's Press, 1981.

Malloy, James M. "Generation of Political Support and Allocation of Costs." In *Revolutionary Change in Cuba*, edited by Carmelo Mesa-Lago, pp. 23–42. Pittsburgh: University of Pittsburgh Press, 1971.

Martz, John. *Central America*. Chapel Hill: University of North Carolina Press, 1959.

Menjívar, R. "Los Problemas del Mundo Rural." In *Centroamérica: Hoy*, edited by E. Torres-Rivas, K. G. Rosenthal, E. Lizano, R. Menjívar, and S. Ramírez, pp. 236–278. Mexico City: Siglo Veintiuno Editores, 1975.

Mesa-Lago, Carmelo. *The Economy of Socialist Cuba: A Two Decade Appraisal*. Albuquerque: University of New Mexico Press, 1981.

Ministry of Agriculture and Agrarian Reform (MIDINRA). *Boletín Agrometeorológico Número 130*. Managua: MIDINRA, May 1983.

———. "Costos de Oportunidad de la Producción de Algodón." Managua, 1982. Mimeographed.

———. "Costos de Producción." Managua, 1981. Mimeographed.

———. "Diagnóstico de la Situación de las Políticas Referidas a las Empresas del APP." Managua, 1982. Mimeographed.

———. Diagnóstico de la Situación del Sector." Managua, 1982. Mimeographed.

———. "La Generación Neta de Divisas del Sector Agrícola y Agroindustrial de Exportación." Managua, 1982. Mimeographed.

———. *Marco Jurídico de la Reforma Agraria Nicaragüense*. Managua: MIDINRA, 1982.

———. "La Política de Salarios, de Organización y de Normas del Trabajo." Managua, 1982. Mimeographed.

———. "La Política para los Productores Capitalistas." Managua, 1982. Mimeographed.

———. "Las Políticas para el Sector Agropecuario; Presentación por Subsistemas Productivos." Managua, 1982. Mimeographed.

———. "Subsistema del Café." Managua, 1982. Mimeographed.

———. "Subsistema de Maíz y Frijol." Managua, 1982. Mimeographed.

Ministry of Planning (MIPLAN). *Programa Económico de Austeridad y Eficiencia 81*. Managua: MIPLAN, 1981.

Mittleman, James H. "The Dialectic of National Autonomy and Global Participation: Alternatives to Conventional Strategies of Development—Mozambique Experience." *Alternatives* 5 (November 1979): 307–328.

Monteforte, M. *Centro America*. Mexico City: Universidad Nacional Autónoma de México, 1972.

Morawetz, David. "Economic Lessons from Some Small Socialist Develop-
    ing Countries." *World Development* 8 (May-June 1980): 337–369.
National Bank of Nicaragua. "Costos de Producción." Managua, 1978.
    Mimeographed.
————. *Estudio de la Economía del Algodón en Nicaragua*. Managua: Na-
    tional Bank of Nicaragua, 1965.
National Secretary for Propaganda and Political Education, FSLN. *Programa
    de Reactivación Económica en Beneficio del Pueblo*. Managua: National
    Secretary for Propaganda and Political Education, FSLN, 1980.
Nuñez, Orlando. *El Somocismo y el Modelo Capitalista Agroexportador*. Ma-
    nagua: Dept. de Ciencias Sociales de la Universidad Nacional Autónoma
    de Nicaragua, 1981.
Ottaway, Marina, and Ottaway, David. *Ethiopia*. New York: Africana Pub-
    lishing Company, 1978.
Petras, James F., and Morley, Morris H. "Economic Expansion, Political Cri-
    sis and U.S. Policy in Central America." *Contemporary Marxism* 3 (Sum-
    mer 1981): 71–88.
Radu, Michael S. "Mozambique: Nonalignment or New Dependence?" *Cur-
    rent History* 83 (March 1984): 101–104, 132–135.
Rodríguez, Mario. *Central America*. Englewood Cliffs, N.J.: Prentice-Hall,
    1965.
Scott, James C. *Everyday Forms of Peasant Resistance*. New Haven, Conn.:
    Yale University Press, forthcoming.
Seligson, Mitchell. *Peasants of Costa Rica and the Development of Agrarian
    Capitalism*. Madison: University of Wisconsin Press, 1980.
Sequeira, Carlos Guillermo. "State and Private Marketing Arrangements in
    the Agricultural Export Industries: The Case of Nicaragua's Coffee and
    Cotton." Ph.D. dissertation, Harvard University, 1981.
Small and Medium Agricultural Producers of Nicaragua (UNAG). *Plan de
    Lucha*. Managua: MIDINRA, 1981.
Superior Council of Private Enterprise (COSEP). *Análisis Sobre la Ejecución
    del Programa de Gobierno de Reconstrucción Nacional*. Managua: CO-
    SEP, 1980.
Sutton, Keith. "The Progress of Algeria's Agrarian Reform and Its Settlement
    Implications." *Maghreb Review* 3 (January-April 1978): 10–15.
Sweezy, Paul M. *Post-Revolutionary Society*. New York: Monthly Review
    Press, 1980.
Swetnam, John J. "Disguised Employment and Development Policy in Peas-
    ant Economies." *Human Organization* 39 (Spring 1980): 32–39.
Union of Nicaraguan Agricultural Producers (UPANIC). "Costos de la Reno-
    vación del Café." Managua, 1982. Mimeographed.
————. "Estudios Económicos." Managua, 1983. Mimeographed.

United Nations Institute for Social Development. *Food Systems and Society: The Case of Nicaragua*. Geneva: United Nations Institute for Social Development, 1981.

Uphoff, Norman. "Political Considerations in Human Development." In *Implementing Programs of Human Development, World Bank Staff Working Paper No. 403*, pp. 1–82. Washington, D.C.: World Bank, 1980.

Uzzell, J. Douglas. "Mixed Strategies and the Informal Sector: Three Faces of Reserve Labor." *Human Organization* 39 (Spring 1980): 40–49.

Valenzuela, Arturo. *Chile*. Baltimore: Johns Hopkins University Press, 1978.

Velázquez P., Alvaro F. "Estudio Comparativo Sobre la Problemática de la Producción Algodonera Entre los Ciclos Agrícolas 77/78 y 82/83." Lic. thesis, Instituto Tecnológico y de Estudios Superiores de Monterrey, 1983.

Walker, Thomas W. *Nicaragua*. Boulder, Colo.: Westview Press, 1981.

Warnken, Philip. *The Agricultural Development of Nicaragua*. Columbia: University of Missouri Press, 1975.

Weber, Henri. *Nicaragua: The Sandinista Revolution*. London: Verso Editions, 1981.

Wheelock, Jaime. *Imperialismo y Dictadura*. Mexico City: Siglo Veintiuno Editores, 1979.

———. *Nicaragua: Imperialismo y Dictadura*. Havana: Editorial de Ciencias Sociales, 1980.

White, Gordon. "Revolutionary Socialist Development in the Third World: An Overview." In *Revolutionary Socialist Development in the Third World*, edited by Gordon White, Robin Murray, and Christine White, pp. 1–34. London: Wheatsheaf Books, 1983.

Woodward, Ralph, Jr. *Central America*. New York: Oxford University Press, 1976.

World Bank. *The Economic Development of Nicaragua*. Baltimore: Johns Hopkins University Press, 1959.

Nicaraguan Newspapers and Magazines

Barricada
El Nuevo Diario
Encuentro
La Prensa
Patria Libre

Index

Africa, post-revolutionary regimes and economies in, 8, 62–63, 83–84

"African socialism," 63

Agrarian reform: Nicaraguan state policy of, 85–86, 91, 108; in post-revolutionary regimes, 21–22. *See also* Agriculture and Agrarian Reform, Ministry of; Land access; Land tenure

Agrarian Reform, Ministry of. *See* Agriculture and Agrarian Reform, Ministry of

Agrarian Reform Law (1981), 91

Agricultural production: by form of ownership, 42 (table), 43–44; Nicaraguan dependence on, 24, 25, 29; under Somoza, 31–33; state role in, 43–44. *See also* Exports; State farms; *and names of specific crops and forms of production*

Agriculture and Agrarian Reform, Ministry of (MIDINRA), 6, 36, 79, 111; and cooperatives, 89; on costs of coffee production, 71–72; formation of, 36, 43; and land access program, 108; and state credit policy, 90; and welfare of wage labor, 104

Agrochemical industry, 33

Algeria, post-revolutionary economic problems in, 14, 19, 21

Allende, Salvador, 2, 9, 14, 17

Angola, 129

Arce, Bayardo, 37, 40

Association of Rural Workers (ATC), 106, 108

Atlantic coast region, 26, 29–30, 116

Balance of payments problems, 20, 122. *See also* Exports; Foreign trade

Banana production, 30

Banking system, 123, 124

Barricada: on problem of basic grain prices, 97–98; on renovated farms, 82

Basic grains. *See* Grains, basic; *and names of specific crops*

Bates, Robert H., on state marketing agencies in Africa, 63, 83

Bean production, 5, 86, 95, 102; area cultivated and yield for, 98–100, 99 (table); by form of ownership, 42 (table). *See also* Grains, basic

Beef exports, 124, 125 (table). *See also* Cattle production; Livestock production

Block committees (CDSs), 38

Bluefields (Zelaya department), 113, 115

Boaco department, 105

Bolivia: Nationalist Revolutionary movement in, 2; nationalizations in, 14; price increases in, 17; private-sector concessions made in, 20; and vulnerability of post-revolutionary regime, 23

Brazil, coffee production in, 68

Brinton, Crane, on definition of revolution, 9

Bulgaria, aid to Nicaragua from, 2, 121

Burnham, Forbes, 23

Cabral, Amílcar, 23

Cacao production, 28

Canada, 12; aid to Nicaragua from, 130 (table)

Compositor:	Wilsted & Taylor
Text:	10/12 Times Roman
Display:	Goudy
Printer:	Edwards Brothers, Inc.
Binder:	Edwards Brothers, Inc.